Think Ahead
Stay Ahead

Think Ahead Stay Ahead

WHAT EVERY LEADER NEEDS TO KNOW

In knowledge partnership with **hindustantimes**

RUPA

Published by
Rupa Publications India Pvt. Ltd 2016
7/16, Ansari Road, Daryaganj
New Delhi 110002

Sales Centres:

Allahabad Bengaluru Chennai
Hyderabad Jaipur Kathmandu
Kolkata Mumbai

ISBN: 978-81-291-4232-0

First impression 2016

10 9 8 7 6 5 4 3 2 1

Typeset by Saanvi Graphics, Noida

Contents

x

CONTENTS

Publisher's Note

In this compilation, India's best and brightest business leaders present their leadership ideas, concepts and models. Interviewed from 2012–2014, some of these leaders have moved on to other roles from the ones mentioned here.

'Leadership is giving people enough space': KEKI MISTRY,

VICE-CHAIRMAN, CEO, HDFC

A three-decade veteran at mortgage lender Housing Development Finance Corporation (HDFC), in what is only his second job—the first being with Tatas promoted Indian Hotels—Keki Mistry, has played a critical role in the lenders transformation into India's leading financial services company that also dabbles in banking, asset management and insurance. Leadership, he says, is about having the courage to take responsibility when there's a goof-up and also about not interfering in others' work. Excerpts from an interview:

How would you define leadership?

Leadership is acceptance. It is not forcing others to do things your way but giving people enough space.

What are the qualities of a good leader?

A leader must have a clear vision of what the organization needs to do. He should be able to articulate and make people understand the vision. The vision must be translated into corporate goals that must be well defined and capable of being measured. A leader must be approachable to his colleagues. He should be willing to listen to suggestions and should not impose his ideas on others. A leader must be able to take decisions. He must accept his mistake in case of wrong decisions. This brings a feeling of transparency to his staff. He should be lavish while praising colleagues for a job well done.

Which kind of leadership style is best?

Leadership styles could be different. You can have a leader who likes to be hands-on and wants to know every detail of what is going on in the organization. Another style is to adopt a hands-off approach, ensuring that corporate goals are met in an ethical manner without getting involved in micro management. It's not that one quality is good and the other is bad, you can have equally successful leaders using different styles.

What is your leadership style?

My preference is to be a little hands-off. If you start getting into every detail, then you are interfering in others work. The two most important things are creating an atmosphere where your staff does not fear to come to office on Monday and have a transparent policy.

What leadership advice would you give to your daughter?

I would suggest that she learns from people around her. Also, I would tell her to never lose sleep over something since things do not always go your way.

What is your leadership advice to young professionals?

Patience and integrity is key. They should not aspire to become a leader the next day. As you learn, pick your way up in life and you will automatically develop leadership qualities. Not every decision you take will be correct. Admit those mistakes. Every person has the potential to become a leader.

Can a manager become a leader?

Yes, you need to be someone who has learnt his way up, understands the work, keeps an open mind and gives flexibility to people. As managers grow they understand corporate goals, the organization's culture and automatically become a leader. There is nothing like a born leader.

How do you nurture leadership at HDFC?

At HDFC we try to create an environment where we can identify good people and entrust them with greater responsibilities so that they can be tested out under different conditions. In a few cases, we have even moved some of our people to head other businesses that we have undertaken. We believe that an individual who joins the organization has a lot to contribute to the long-term goal. He should be willing to be in the organization for a long period, not someone who looks at HDFC as a stepping stone.

SACHIN KUMAR

'To be a leader, you don't need an MBA': HARI SHANKAR SINGHANIA,

PRESIDENT, JK ORGANIZATION

The scion of a business family from Kanpur, the late Hari Shankar Singhania, began his career in Calcutta when he was all of 18. He shifted his base to Delhi in the 70s and was the president of the 100-year-old JK Organization, a group of diversified companies. Known for his entrepreneurial abilities and his pioneering ventures, Singhania, a Padma Bhushan awardee, shared his views on leadership and business ethics. Excerpts:

JK Organization, whose roots go back a hundred years, began purely as a family-run business and transformed into a multi-product, multi-location and multi-business industrial group. How did you transform your leadership style from a traditional one to a modern corporate outlook?

The transformation took place through evolution. In the past our aim was one of self reliance—producing goods and delivering services that were then imported as per government policy. As the economy expanded and got liberalized, our aim also changed. From the domestic market, we wanted to go global and change our style of functioning too. The focus was on innovation in a big way. For instance, we were the ones to introduce radial tyres in India.

Do you agree that in a family run business, there is hardly any decentralization in vertical leadership, and it is more about control by an individual?

I cannot comment on others. As far as our group is concerned, family members have become professionals. Each company has qualified professionals at the level of COO. They are all on the board. You began your business career at 18 and through your entrepreneurial capabilities, have set up various pioneering ventures in India.

What defines a true entrepreneur?

A true entrepreneur spots business opportunities before others can. When you analyse opportunities, do not get carried away by emotions. You should have a far-sighted approach. Above all, one has to have clarity of vision and goal. Let nothing deter you from this path.

Who has influenced you the most as a leader in your work field?

I have been influenced and inspired by a large number of persons, but it was my uncle Sir Padampatji and my father Lala Lakshmipatji who influenced me the most. They achieved many things despite difficult conditions and uncertainties, and taught me what leadership is all about.

What would you consider to be your best leadership decision?

Shifting my base from Calcutta to New Delhi in the late 70s, when West Bengal was on the precipice of deindustrialization and flight of capital. And industrialization was spreading its wings in the north—the political & economic powerbase of India.

And your worst business decision?

In the early 80s, the shackles of control and regulations were being loosened and we the indigenous entrepreneurs were getting a taste of freedom, perhaps for the first time since Independence, in business. Many entrepreneurs were getting into reckless diversification in areas that were seemingly perceived as profitable and like many of our peers, we too had diversified into several areas of what you call today 'non-core businesses'. It ultimately couldn't survive the turbulence of incoming-competition and failed to pursue the changing market. But as I look back, we were learning by committing mistakes and consolidating with wisdom.

As a leader, how difficult was it to steer your companies during the licence-permit raj and more recently, at a time when the economy is slowing down?

During the licence permit raj, one used to get notice for producing more than the licenced quota, unlike today. It was a different time. During adversities we steered with our experiences and focussed on the fact that life goes on as the business goes on.

You had been a president of both FICCI and the International Chamber of Commerce (Paris). How far can industry chambers act as catalysts in influencing governments decisions?

Chambers are social institutions and not just business lobbies. They have to play a proactive role in policy formation, like FICCI takes up issues on behalf of industry with policy-makers. At the International Chamber of Commerce, we initiated the process of globalization in a successful manner. Moreover, a businessman should first nurture his own organization and abide by the consensus worked out in these forums; otherwise he can't command respect from either the government or the public.

During your 15 years as chairman of the governing body of IIM, Lucknow, a couple of centres of excellence were created. How would you define 'excellence' ?

I strongly believe that 'excellence' comes from an urge to strive and deliver the best every time. It is a mindset that says, 'When it is good enough, improve it.'

It is also a way of thinking and passion that comes only from a drive within. Despite not being an MBA, you emerged as one of the most successful and respected corporate leaders. How was it possible? Do you think an MBA degree really matters in inculcating leadership quality in an individual?

An MBA degree is helpful. But to be a leader, you don't need an MBA. What is important is vision, hard work, ability to accept challenges, take right decisions and to ensure that there is no trust deficit.

What about business ethics? What should a corporate leader follow?

One should accept that economic development is for the people, for the society at large, and the consumer in particular. Above all, in a country where nearly half the population lives below poverty line, overall growth by itself is not enough. It must find meaningful expression in the day-to-day life of the common man. Emphasis should be on addressing the unemployment issue and create jobs in both urban and rural areas, and on rural development.

DEBOBRAT GHOSE

'Being yourself is the best way to be a good leader': HARISH MANWANI,

NON-EXECUTIVE CHAIRMAN, HUL AND COO, UNILEVER

Leadership, and leaders by extension, cannot exist in a vacuum and can only survive if there are followers who feel a genuine connect with the leader, feels Harish Manwani, COO, Unilever and non-executive chairman, HUL, in an interview. Excerpts:

How would you define leadership?

It has a few dimensions. The first is that leaders need followers. If you are a leader who believes you are setting the pace, and then look back and see that no one's following you, you got a big problem. I can say this because I have been a leader and I have been a follower.

So how do you build a following?

To build followership, you need to do a few things right. First, you have to have a sense of destination. Leaders always give companies a sense of destination. As leaders you must be connected with your people and the society in which you operate because otherwise you will not have a point of view. Look at millions of political leaders who lost it because they were not connected—business is the same. I don't go to a single market unless I have spent half a day visiting shops—that's my job. See how people are buying, what are they doing, talk to the customers, go to retailers. Then I go to consumer homes—so you have to remain connected. The third point about leadership is values. There is something non-negotiable that you have to define. If you don't have any non-negotiables, you are an unanchored ship.

Does that mean leaders have to be intransigent?

You must have all the flexibility, all the dynamic source planning and everything else, but at the end of the day, you have to anchor your company with some non-negotiable values, and what you stand for.

How do these qualities play out in your leadership style?

I believe that being authentic, and being yourself is the best way to be a good leader. A lot of people try to mimic leadership. Be yourself—that's the best thing you can do. When I walk into my office at HUL or Unilever, I am not a different person inside the company as I am outside.

Why is leadership so important today?

Because there is a big value now, on what I call the fourth dimension of growth. We have defined a firm's agenda in terms of consistent, competitive and profitable growth. I believe that a very important fourth dimension, in terms of leadership is now responsible growth.

So is it lack of responsible growth that has caused the failure of the entire leadership?

First of all it would be wrong to say that the entire leadership has failed. Just because there is a part of the corporate world, the financial world, where we had the kind of things that should not have happened, does not mean that every single leader has dropped their standards. It's just that we are going through a time where the extent of damage done by irresponsible leadership, has overpowered anything good happening.

Do you feel today there is a rising enquiry among press and regulators on the leadership issue? Do you feel more watched?

I don't feel so but I know that we live in a world where we have to always hold a mirror to ourselves. Therefore we have to be even more exemplary in the way we behave and come across.

What is the process of a manager becoming a leader—are there born leaders?

I think it's a bit of a theoretical discussion about whether leaders are born or made. If you take the corporate world, there is a hardware dimension of leadership that you need to have and you acquire—which is all about functional expertise, experience, learning how to take good decisions and analytics. Then there's a software—about the ability to have a point of view, to be authentic. The transition happens as you grow up in the organization and you move from managing businesses to ensuring management of businesses. That is where your growing up process starts and I think there's no such thing as born leaders.

TEJEESH N.S. BEHL

'A true leader is somebody with a vision': YVES CARCELLE,

CEO, LOUIS VUITTON

The late Yves Carcelle was the chairman & CEO of Louis Vuitton, the most successful brand of the $26 billion French luxury conglomerate LVMH. He was also seen by many as the leader among leaders in the world of luxury. He had shared his views on leadership. Excerpts:

Who according to you is a true leader?

Well, a true leader is someone with a vision. But then, the vision cannot be achieved unless it percolates down to the colleagues in the organization. Once it is done then comes the setting up of objectives to effectively implement that vision. Once the objectives are set, then validate and prioritize and lead the team to achieving that vision. There are many successful leaders in their respective fields and each one is different in their approach.

In the world of luxury, you are considered the leader among all chairmen, presidents and CEO, yet you are also seen as someone who keeps close proximity with his employees, to the extent that you even know the names of the doormen as much as the country managers of the 460 stores you have in several countries… Every employee loves you… Comments?

What I am to my colleagues and how I interact with them is something that I have within me, my actions are not deliberate. I am made that way and I love to interact with people. If that contributes to the overall growth of my brand then I am happy. I am also happy that I am loved. But then you can run a family with love, not the company you work for. I have had occasions where I had to terminate dozens of colleagues who did not perform to my expectations. I believe that if someone is not performing, one should do the favour of making him aware of that fact and help them pursue something where s/he can fare better, rather than keep pushing the person for long and at the end make him or her unproductive, and then realize the time wasted.

To what do you attribute the success of Louis Vuitton?

As I told you what is important is to have a vision. In 1854, the founder, Louis Vuitton, started his venture with a vision. He wanted to conquer the world right from the start and worked hard towards it throughout his life…making things that are unique and then reinventing them as he went along. Today, Louis Vuitton does exactly the same, reinventing, rebuilding the brand as we go along.

Where the connoisseur treads, others follow. Whether it is a country, or a location in a country, it is believed that most brands wait till you make your entry and then they follow you… What makes your brand the leader of the world of luxury?

Well, this is nothing new. We were the first to enter the UK market when we set up our first store in London in 1885… It was the first

Louis Vuitton overseas store. Then many countries followed and now we have several stores all across the world. We were the first to enter India in 2003…now with Chennai, we have five stores in this country. We look at all aspects very carefully before entering a country or location and we are happy if we are followed wherever we go. We always look forward to achieving the missions set and look ahead in rebuilding our brand, as our founder did in 1854.

But then, you do all the planning and then decide to go to a location and when others follow you there…doesn't it irk you that they are enjoying the fruits of your labour?

No. On the contrary I am happy we have their company wherever we go. I much rather have the company of luxury brands with similar profiles than a rug dealer next to my store. Besides, I always liked healthy competition. Like-minded brands being next to each other will also improve the overall conditions that are important for a luxury retail environment. Luxury is all about passion and living in it, the more they come close to where we are the merrier it gets for us.

How did Louis Vuitton manage to make profits even during the worst global financial conditions?

Every time when there was a recession, our brand kept moving forward. I think it is all about believing in your brand and never compromising on its quality regardless of the situation you are in. You've got to move forward no matter what. That's what we always did. Of course, along the way one has got to be careful. Those who love real luxury will always go for it regardless of the times.

Now comes the best and the worst part… As a leader, what is the best decision that you have taken for Louis Vuitton?

I think one of the best decisions that I have taken for the brand, of course along with LVMH chairman Bernard Arnault, was to bring

American designer Marc Jacobs in as our artistic director in order to rebuild the brand. It worked very well for us. He brought in his vision in design and it pushed the brand further. Also, my decision to enter the Chinese market…it was taken at the right time in 1991 and today we have 41 stores in various part of China.

…And the worst?

Worst I would say is not about a decision taken…it is about a decision that I did not take! Perhaps I should have paid more attention towards exotic skins, controlling and sourcing, way before than we did… Now for the last few years we are at it and it is working well for us.

VINOD NAIR

'A good leader leads like he would be led': SHANTANU PRAKASH,

FOUNDER AND MD, EDUCOMP SOLUTIONS LIMITED

Shantanu Prakash founded Educomp Solutions Limited in 1994, a few years after graduating from the Indian Institute of Management, Ahmedabad, with the vision to 'transform the teaching-learning process through the use of technology and best practices.' Prakash borrowed Rs 1 lakh from his father, and began an enterprise by setting up computer labs in schools. Educomp, which featured in Forbes' 'Best under a billion' list last year, currently employs over 16,000 people across 27 offices worldwide including India, Canada, Nigeria, Saudi Arabia and Singapore working with over 26,000 schools and 15 million students. He spoke on a range of issues on leadership. Excerpts:

How do you define a leader?

Anyone who sticks his neck out; who says he can do it when everyone else evades; anyone who takes responsibility, is a leader. Applied to business, a leader would have these same traits but with an entrepreneurial passion that he or she brings to any work that he/she chooses, or is given. Anybody who stands by his work, irrespective of success or failure, and who is willing to admit and learn from his mistakes, and one who refuses to give up easily, is a leader in my view.

What is your leadership mantra?

Lead like you would be led. A leader must always remember that his greatest asset are human resources and that he is dealing with people who have the same instincts as he does—so whether it is reward and incentive, pressure and stress, application and diligence, or focus and concentration, he has to acknowledge that everybody broadly ticks the same way. Accordingly, you have to nurture these qualities or strengthen or adjust them in accordance with the personalities you are dealing with and in relation to the objectives that must be achieved. At senior levels, I believe our function is more about moderating and modulating the energies of our team leaders so that they can achieve more that they themselves think they can. Guiding is the primary work of leaders.

How do you cultivate leaders?

My style is to put people to the challenge and let the results speak for themselves. The best way to test someone's mettle is to give them the tools they need, agree on the outcomes, give them the space and freedom, and then let them show you if they can do it or not. That is the only way to pick winners. No amount of theoretical estimation can provide what proof of work can and so what we can do is to encourage and support until they find their own genius for solving problems and leading from the front.

You have also undergone a management course at IIM, Ahmedabad. So, according to you, can leadership be taught or is it ingrained in a person?

Leadership is not a title, it is an attitude. So, some of it must be ingrained in your character and a lot of it can be processed to iron out the wrinkles. That is where education and training come into play. Streamlining a basic aptitude or honing God-given skills are part of any developmental process. So, if a manager wants to extend his training into entrepreneurial zeal he is better placed with a background preparation—which only a specialist institution can provide.

As a leader are you a consensus builder or top-down guy?

A bit of both, actually. I believe it is necessary to have a clear vision about objectives, methods and direction. Outside of that, a good leaders must ensure that everyone buys into the mechanics of the process. To agree on an outcome but have disagreements on the way to achieve it would be counterproductive, so the two must move in tandem. Clarity of direction, the sanctity of operational values, and overall consensus are necessary to actualize any initiative.

What has been your best leadership decision?

To branch out on my own has been my best decision. Although I did it with very little experience in the field I chose and learnt on the job, the fact remains that we were in a nascent industry and there was very little established knowledge on the business at the point. So, while I do emphasize the importance of domain expertise, in my case it worked to my advantage. This was because our learning became our USP and provided us a huge IP leverage over competitors, thanks to the original and pioneering work we were forced to do in the field.

...And your worst decision?

Though I can't say I was the only one, but not reading the economic slowdown or its severity has to be a close miss. It came at a point when we were invested to grow our businesses in newer directions and it distracted us from our estimations. However, I guess we have to rough it out like everyone else until the outlook improves. The good part though is that this period has allowed us to look at our businesses more critically, in terms of administration and management, costs and making us much more efficient in terms of productivity and returns. It has also enabled us to recast expansion, consolidate and reposition ourselves for a future thrust.

Name two leaders you admire the most.

Mahatma Gandhi and Sri Sri Ravi Shankar.

GAURAV CHOUDHURY

'A leader can't allow ego to dictate decisions': AJAY PIRAMAL,

CHAIRMAN, PIRAMAL HEALTHCARE

Flush with cash from the sale of his generic drugs business to Abbott Laboratories in 2010, Ajay Piramal, chairman, Piramal Healthcare, has been identifying opportunities to put his billions into profitable use, for himself as well as his shareholders, for as he says, a leader needs to be smart enough to see a good deal when it comes his way, and cash in on it. Excerpts:

How do you view your role as a leader—is it being a savvy investor or is it more of a turnaround specialist?

I have an obligation to my shareholders, to create maximum value for whatever they have invested and that's what my job is and that's what I am here to deliver. I don't carry an egoistic or emotional attachment to the businesses. We did a calculation to justify the value that Abbott paid—I would have had to grow the business for 15 years at 20% CAGR with an operating margin in excess of 35%. Now that's not possible and therefore, the choice was should I leave aside my ego that it is my business and I created it, or should I do what is in the best interest of the shareholders. If you look at like that, that's what a leader ought to do, in my view. Job of a leader is to act like a trustee.

But trustee has to be smart enough to recognize the opportunity, because at the end of the day there is also a personal benefit that you get?

Yes, because I am a shareholder so I will get that.

What are the essential qualities for a leader?

A good leader has to have high integrity. Integrity means what you think, what you say and what you do should be in alignment. To me a good leader must be courageous—courage to take decisions. To me a good leader is somebody who is dispassionate and doesn't get carried away.

Do you think you have imbibed all these attributes or are you falling short somewhere?

I don't know. I am falling short in many places.

For example?

I don't think I like to spend as much time on execution detail and in system processes. I also think I am sometimes too soft with people when one has to take harsh decisions.

Could you shed some light on your failures as a leader?

We failed sometimes in terms of some acquisitions. For example, after we acquired bulk drug unit in Hyderabad, for many years it was bleeding. That was a wrong decision or we did not assess it properly.

Then why did you stick with it and not exit?

Because there was no choice, otherwise you have to write it off.

So you are not prepared to take failures in your stride?

No, I have no problem. I mean so many times we fail and you have to fail. If you have not failed then I think you have not taken enough risk. So failure is part of life and that in some way strengthens you.

How would you go about the deal again, if given a second chance?

First, the selection of target is very important and here, I believe integrity is really important. The person you are dealing with should have high ethical standards. I think that is a mistake we made, for instance in Hyderabad, we did not do enough diligence on the person who sold it to us, he said something and delivered something else. Second, in an acquisition one has to be decisive, one must have a clear plan what he wants to do and then act accordingly. About 70% of the mergers fail because of the ego of the chief executive saying I want to do it, and then I don't care for value or anything.

Has your role as a leader become challenging as you increase your presence in other countries?

The way to run business is changing, more employees out of India, more senior people now, more diversified businesses, you don't know as much, if it is one or two businesses you can understand, here your knowledge is limited, so yes it is more challenging. So we are adapting, we are changing.

Can you elaborate how you are changing?

One is that now we are pushing down much more full responsibility of a business to individuals and giving them more authority. They are accountable for delivering results. Earlier I used to have that responsibility. Also, getting high quality of people means incentivizing them in the manner which you haven't done earlier, through stock options.

SACHIN KUMAR AND TEJEESH N.S. BEHL

'Leadership is thinking out of the box': UDAY KOTAK,

VICE-CHAIRMAN & MD, KOTAK MAHINDRA BANK

One of India's 48 billionaires—the latest Forbes rich list ranks him at 270 with a net worth of $4.1 billion—Uday Kotak, vice-chairman and managing director, Kotak Mahindra Bank, says leadership is about being disruptive and thinking out of the box. Excerpts from an interview:

What would be the defining trait of leadership, according to you?

Leadership is building a team having a common purpose, and executing that purpose. It is about identifying an opportunity in advance and most of the times people see it after it's gone. For example, nobody saw an opportunity in tablets but Steve Jobs. Even the consumers do not know that they have a need. So when an opportunity flows most people ignore it. And once you get that opportunity, your ability to execute it—that is the key difference between success and failure. There are many visionaries but success is with the person who executes that vision. People underestimate the importance of execution.

How do you identify opportunity and execute it?

You have to follow your own instinct. Humans have a tendency to think that it is too risky, or I can't do that. In India we have two diseases, what I call 'needling' and 'tolding'. You ask any manager and he will say: We need to do this—in that case, why don't you do this? And second is: Telling—I have told him, or passed on the work to someone else. Why have you told him, why haven't you done that yourself?

What is your leadership style?

I like to build consensus, but once I'm clear about something then I decide. I try to carry my team along but I am not scared to take a decision if it is not popular. I also think leadership should not be predictable. If it's too predictable then people know that if they behave in a particular manner, then the boss will react in a set way. But unpredictability does not imply inconsistency—you have to be consistent in your philosophy but must have the ability to think out of the box.

Any such instance of unpredictability you can recount?

It was not an easy decision for us to buy back the Goldman Sachs stake in 2006. The predictable thing was to sell out but we finally looked deep inside and went with our conviction—which brings us to another important issue about leadership. That the line between conviction and foolhardiness is very thin.

Has the job of a leader become tough in times of a slowdown, especially when he has to take a decision on downsizing?

Every downturn is an opportunity because if you have the right strategy and you execute it right, then post-downturn you have chances of getting a higher market share. But often employees are the last to know about developments.

Is that due to a lack of respect or is the leader too scared to tell the truth?

I think it is both. It is extremely important to carry your team in good and bad times. And when leadership does not have the trust of its people, it's a huge sign of weakness of the firm. The two most important constituents of any firm are customers and employees. With both these categories, I put disproportionate importance to trust. Conduct of a person builds trust, and trust is fragile—it has to be nurtured. A firm must give as much importance to internal communication as to external communication.

So where do most leaders go wrong?

Most of the times people struggle on the 'who' and lose the sight of 'what'. It is not about who is right, but what is right. Stick to the principle of what is right and manage the who separately.

Which historical leader do you admire most and why?

Mahatma Gandhi, he was the smartest negotiator in the world. What negotiating leverage did he have when he went to the queen in a dhoti and yet, he shifted the negotiating leverage in his favour—as if saying that I am half naked because of what you have done to my country. The way Gandhi used fasts as a negotiating leverage, smartly, time and again, that too in an era of no mobiles—he is the one of the smartest negotiators history has seen.

SACHIN KUMAR AND TEJEESH N.S. BEHL

'Leaders should walk the talk': ROBERT S. KAPLAN,

PROFESSOR, HARVARD BUSINESS SCHOOL

Management guru Robert S. Kaplan, credited with innovative practices—ranging from Balanced Scorecard to time-driven Activity-Based Costing—says the most challenging time for a leader is when things go bad. The Marvin Bower Professor of Leadership Development–Emeritus, Harvard Business School (USA) talked about leadership development. Excerpts:

Your Balanced Scorecard was a success. Do you think it's still relevant and will be in the future as well?

It has the permanent approval of managers and managements. Without Balance Scorecard (BS), companies have only financial reporting system. It was fine for 20th century enterprises, where values came from physical aspects such as inventories, retail, etc. But companies today use intangible assets such as customers' loyalty, innovation, etc., for which we need to see beyond the financial system. There is a huge gap between the vision and strategy developed at the top and the people down in an organization. There is a need to bridge the link between strategy and employee empowerment for continuous improvement. BS provides that link.

Often, the most innovative ideas arise first in a business and not in business schools. How can this gap be bridged?

There does exist a gap. The challenge before business schools is to identify innovative practices and capture them. However, business schools and universities are more into academics. The need is to break through the academic barriers.

How important is the role of communication in leadership?

Any leader has to be an effective communicator. If a leader wants to take an organization ahead, or in the case of a leadership change where it is not natural for people often to accept the change—effective communication plays a crucial role.

Often, leaders or frontline managers fail to develop a second line of leadership in an organization. Why?

Probably insecurity and fear are a part of human characteristic. A leader who fails to develop a second line of leadership is not a good leader. The most important role is to develop a successor in an organization. Leaders have to allow themselves to be vulnerable, but not weak. They should allow others to challenge them and should not take punitive action against those who challenge, because it helps in generating ideas.

What basic qualities should a corporate executive have, to be a future leader?

Effective communication, accepting challenges, risk-taking ability, encouraging others to develop and authenticity. Leaders should be able to walk the talk—follow the principles he talks about and reinforce the message he gives to people.

It is said, 'great leaders are born and not made.' Your take?

Not true. Leadership qualities can be nurtured through training, through specific career assignments, new challenges, new businesses and new regions and culture. We have to reinforce the traits within people, teach them through cases, and influence their thinking.

Can business schools groom leaders?

A strong commitment is needed for that and depends on faculty members. For example, former chief executive officer (CEO) of Medtronic, William George, who penned *Authentic Leadership* joined Harvard Business School faculty after retirement. Within five years, the elective course he was teaching became the most popular one, with 75% students opting for it.

How important is the role of a corporate leader during slowdown or chaos?

The most challenging time for a leader is when things go bad. A great leader gives hope. If people find the leader discouraged, they stop working. A leader should be the one who is able to inspire others in adversities.

What has been your best leadership decision?

During one of my first assignments at Carnegie Mellon University, I was asked to teach accounts, which I didn't study. But I could do it well and I realized that I had a flair for accounts and I was unaware of it. I used my quantitative skills in research and teaching. After 15 years when I switched over to HBS, the same was used to develop new practices in business research.

And the worst?

May be the decision to become dean at Carnegie Mellon for six years. My functioning was more administrative than scholastic. But it exposed me to business practices, which otherwise wouldn't have been possible.

And your leadership mantra?

I have a simple message. Measurement plays an important role in the management system and I devised it. Often frontline employees or middle managers don't understand what leaders communicate with them on high-level strategy and vision. A leader has to ensure that his employees understand the strategy better through measurable objectives, so that it can be translated into local action. And take a position, do the work you love and don't regret it.

'A leader changes as organization grows': HARSH C. MARIWALA,

CMD, MARICO

His management style has evolved through years of hands-on experience of leading his company, a style which has filled in nicely for the absence of a management degree on his curriculum vitae. However, that hasn't stopped him from devouring management books, just to be on the same page as his senior MBA-armed managers, says Harsh C. Mariwala, chairman and managing director, Marico, in an interview. Experts:

How would you define a leader?

A leader should create a long-term sustainable model of success for the organization. Even if he is not there tomorrow, the organization should run—to me that's a great leader. You've seen that many leaders, when they are there, the organization does great, but once they leave, the whole organization falls apart. That kind of a leader has more of yes-men.

How would you define your own style?

It would definitely be one of consensus, delegative but with a broad direction—my job is to see the direction for the organization because we want to be, in whatever we do, in the leadership position.

But were you always like that as a leader, or have you evolved?

I have evolved. Earlier, I was more directive because at that time the focus was growth. But now it is to build consensus, drive a few initiatives within the organization and not control, but to add value. Over a period of time, my style has become more catalytic, more influential. Maybe I was little more impulsive then and impatient—I am still impatient.

So change in leadership style is imperative?

Yes, I think the role of a leader changes as the organization grows. As an entrepreneur, leadership means doing things because you're a small organization. And then from then on, if you become a medium-sized organization, you have to get things done. And when you grow still bigger—from small to medium to large—you have to influence things.

In your journey as a leader, have you made wrong judgements?

There have been many—either chasing a wrong business or underestimating a challenge. We bought a company in the US, it dealt in ayurvedic products and services and supplying to all the spas in the US (Sundari skin care products, which Marico bought in 2003 and sold in 2009). It was a small company and I thought we would leverage our knowledge of ayurveda and make it big in the US but our business model has always been B2C and that business was B2B and we were not able to get the scale. Hence, we sold it off. In another instance, we went into Saffola snack, but the snacks distribution business is quite different from managing a personal products business. However, it taught us a lot and we have now launched a breakfast cereal, under the Saffola brand name. The lessons from that failure have really helped us.

What do you look for when hiring talent for a potential leadership position?

The first thing I look for is how capable that person is in that role and whether he is better than the earlier incumbent. Number two, you also have to look at the leadership style of that person especially at senior levels, because you have built a certain culture in the organization and you don't want a leader who will practice a leadership style that is completely different because that will destroy the culture of the organization. Then, it's very important to have the right values—there are some basic values such as financial integrity which is almost a given, but it's about overall intellectual integrity, because we don't want people to play games in the organization. So you look at that, you look at his past record and then his ambition level because you want persons who have a burning desire to succeed.

Do you agree with the perception that corporate leadership in today's era takes greater recourse to poor economic environment to cover up for their own failure to lead successfully?

It all depends on what kind of industry you are in and to what extent you are dependent on government support. So if you're in an industry, which is heavily controlled, for example infrastructure or telecom, or which requires environmental clearance then a lot will depend on what happens at the government level. Having said that, if you are in a sector which is less regulatory, then it is the CEO's responsibility to chart out the future and not to go on blaming the environment.

TEJEESH N.S. BEHL

'People are still the key to any business': KARL SLYM,

MANAGING DIRECTOR, TATA MOTORS

The late Karl Slym, who was Tata Motors' managing director had decades of experience in the car industry including his stint as the India head of General Motors. The first thing that you have to see when you walk into a company, is which plate spins and which plate wobbles, believed Slym. The jovial and friendly MD, who could effortlessly deliver a few lines in Hindi, had tried to overhaul the image of Tata Motors by enhancing customer experience. Excerpts from an interview:

What is your take on heading an Indian company?

When I was here last time, I was heading the Indian arm of a multinational company. This time, I am leading an Indian company, which has an international presence. It is similar in certain ways, but also starkly different in others. It is great to have the experience of having worked in India earlier, on my side. I have worked in other countries as well, so I can bring on board a different perspective that will not only further our domestic business but also give wings to our global aspirations. Of course, at the same time it is important that you don't lose sight of the local culture. Look around and you will see young engineers with plenty of ideas and aspirations. We need to provide them with an opportunity to be entrepreneurial while working in a company. I want to provide a structure to take this entrepreneurial spirit forward in the right direction.

How easy or difficult is it to adapt to a new organization when you come in at a very senior level?

Leadership qualities are practically the same whether you are in one company or another. But of course, depending on the situation, priorities may change. When you walk into a company you have to see which plate spins and which plate wobbles. You have got to look at all your plates—product, engineering, design, manufacturing, people or marketing—and establish your priorities.

How has corporate leadership evolved over the years?

A lot of changes have occurred. However, core values remain the same. When I started out, a manager was expected to be honest, open, helping and good at interacting with others. I don't think those things have changed. You may have more automation and technology to make things faster. But people are still the key to any business.

What is your best decision?

To join Tata Motors. I think it was a bit of a dream to head an Indian company. Not only is the company an Indian icon, but in the process of joining it, I have also gained a mentor called Ratan Tata. I think I am blessed to have been given this opportunity.

And what is your worst?

There are no regrets. You make the best decision based on what you have in mind or in hand. Of course, there are always experiences of taking decisions that seemed best at that time and you really can't have regrets about it later.

How challenging a market is India?

The Indian market has a special feel to it. The latest and greatest products are all expected here. This market has huge potential in both short as well as long-term. However, people want international products to be priced at local rates. That makes it the most exciting, and, at the same time, the most challenging market for an organization to cater to. To elaborate further on the dynamics of the Indian market, the requirement from the product is that it should be of a high quality and, at the same time, it should be available at a price suitable for local pockets. The high consumer demand here pushes manufacturers to figure out how to do that. The way we innovate to meet that kind of a tough mandate provides us with skills that will help our international business as well.

What is your vision for Tata Motors?

Over the short to medium term, we see ourselves as a strong, number two player in the passenger car business. In the long-term, we hope to become the number one player. Our short term strategy is to bring in new products and improve services. Beyond that, we want to delight our customers. Customers are looking for new things, and we need to make sure we continue to refresh our vehicle portfolio. And, in some segments such as utility vehicles where we were not able to grow the market share, we need additional activity. We are an expert in the truck business and will continue to be so, and we intend to retain our leadership. Our engineering and manufacturing capabilities are our pillars of strength and it is all about harnessing the capabilities we already have.

MANU P. TOMS

'With inspiration, you can do the impossible': RONNIE SCREWVALA,

MD, DISNEY UTV

First generation entrepreneur Ronnie Screwvala is a pioneer in the television, entertainment and gaming industry. Screwvala, managing director of Disney UTV, and founder trustee of Swades Foundation, spoke on various aspects of leadership. Excerpts:

How do you define a leader? What are the most important traits of a leader?

A leader has to lead from the front, and lead by example. Most importantly, a great leader must build credibility and trust all around—with colleagues, customers and the public at large. Integrity of thought and word cannot be relegated to second place at any cost. It is also important to inspire, as with inspiration, you can get colleagues and others to turn the impossible into the possible. This is particularly true in times of crisis as at such times, everyone looks up to the leader for answers and solutions.

Can leadership be learnt? In other words, how can a manager become a leader?

Leadership has to come from within, and, if you look at yourself as a manager, then chances are that you may not emerge as a leader. It has to come naturally, instinctively and needs to be embedded in the DNA of the leader. In some ways you can 'learn' or 'train' leadership qualities and how to take charge, but, in my view, real leadership in areas such as entrepreneurship is more of a natural process.

What is the role of a professional leader in a promoter-driven company?

I think a lot is being made, incorrectly, of this 'professional' versus 'promoter' debate. This argument sometimes creates the impression that founders and promoters can never be professionals. I think an optimal combination of a professional leading and a promoter heading an organization can inject dynamism into it. The promoter brings on the table his risk taking ability, pioneering spirit and quick decision-making, backed by action. A professional leader can add to this with sharp execution plans and skills, an unwavering focus on deliverables, in-depth research and a thorough understanding of the consumer and the rigour of a strong review process.

Since September 2008, the world has fallen into a maelstrom of serial crises. What is the role of a leader in these times?

Part of the reason why the world fell into this maelstrom is that a small minority of heads of companies thought they were great leaders and let their perceptions overtake reality. These leaders closed themselves to feedback on ground realities. These are traits every leader should consciously avoid, for these are the precise reasons that cause leaders to fall off the cliff.

Leaders often carry the cross of other's wrong doings and inefficiencies. Take the global banking sector today, for instance. What role can good leadership play to counter balance this image?

Leadership is very individualistic and cannot be generalized. A leader has to be viewed as a distinct entity and cannot make up for the inefficiencies of others. Actually, in each industry, one will see some clear leaders who stand out clearly, demonstrating that it is as much about the individual himself as much it is for the specific sector. Stay the course in your own belief and performance, and that will be noticed and respected.

Who are the leaders who have inspired you?

More than individuals or personalities, there are certain situations that have inspired me. For instance, the 26/11 terrorist attacks in Mumbai, which held out great lessons in leadership. To see the entire management and staff, irrespective of seniority, thinking of every client in the hotel as a guest even at a time of such a grave emergency, was a remarkable lesson in ownership, commitment and pride in your work. This is a direct reflection of great leadership —of leading from the front, of credibility and of standing by your beliefs at all times.

What is the worst decision you have taken as a leader?

Not taking a hard call to pull the plug on something even when all the signs pointed otherwise and not knowing at that moment that it's wiser to cut your losses and walk. This inability to take a tough call when needed can lead to some of the worst decisions.

What is the best decision that you have taken as a leader?

Staying the course clearly is not only one of the most important aspects of a leader, but also the hallmark of a resilient organization. Resilience is the key to long-term success and to being a great leader. Also, it is imperative not to give up when failure knocks, as it will many a time.

GAURAV CHOUDHURY

'Military style of leadership is redundant': MARTIN BRUDERMÜLLER,

VICE-CHAIRMAN, BASF

Second in command of the $97 billion chemical engineering major BASF, with 1,10,000 employees cross more than a hundred countries, Martin Brudermüller, vice-chairman of the German behemoth, says the company is taking deliberate but gradual measures to make its leadership as diverse as possible. He says it is in line with the company's corporate philosophy of transparency and openness with little elbow room for personal egos as the company attempts to make a transition with a leadership that's inclusive rather than autocratic and thus more acceptable to the younger generation of leaders. Excerpts:

Are there specific leadership traits at BASF?

Cooperative, open, responsible and entrepreneurial—CORE— summarizes our values. One important element of our leadership style is diversity. We are trying to capture all the capabilities of people and bring all the different perspective into decision making.

How do you ensure the diversity?

It has all the aspects. It has the aspect of nationality. It has the aspect of gender. It has the aspect of different educational and professional background. You can imagine, as a German company, the German part is a bit over exposed in the company. It will take some time to develop diversity. To safeguard the credibility, you have to give it some time. In the last six years, we have dramatically increased the share of people with local background in the Asia Pacific region. From very much a German driven company we changed into an organization where two-thirds of people in managerial positions are local people. Except one managing director in Japan, all country heads in the region are local.

Would you say then that corporate values differ in terms of geographies?

I think it is very much (dependent on) the person, to have these values and to really live it. If you want to have a kind of corporate culture, everyone in the organization should share the same values. They can be partly flavoured by local culture. But an Indian, Chinese, American and Pakistani share the same ideas and values on how we deal with each other and on treating others with respect.

How do you ensure openness and transparency?

We have open feedback culture. This is very important. One core value is openness. So you should be able to withstand criticism. All our leaders will have to go through what we call a 360 degree evaluation system. They are evaluated not only by the people whom they are reporting to but by those who report to them as well. We do this regularly. At a certain level upwards it is mandatory. This is the only way to ensure that people stay open.

But won't that lead to ego clashes, as generally, senior leadership dislikes being appraised by subordinates?

I think the autocratic style (of leadership) is really over. Young generation particularly does not like the military kind of style. In every large organization, you have responsibilities. You will have a person at the top. I think people don't have a problem with that. But what is important is how a boss is making decisions. We should create an environment where everyone can speak up. People will be happy if they can bring in some personal hue to the final decision even if it is not their idea that finally got accepted. For that reason, I think it is more involving, inclusive leadership style that is widely accepted now.

You mentioned personal hue—does that indicate leadership needs to have an emotional quotient?

We need leaders with higher social and emotional competence, not only let's say just educational qualification. We need people with a more holistic personality. This is the direction the companies should adopt to choose their leaders.

Is that the way you would describe yourself as a leader?

I am definitely not perfect. But I would say I am an open person. I am emotional. I have been with the company for 23 years and I know this company in detail. I know its heartbeat. I am a people person. And I love talking to them.

MANU P. TOMS

'Leadership is a steering that keeps companies going in right direction': RICHARD ALLISON,

EXECUTIVE VP, DOMINO'S PIZZA
INTERNATIONAL

Domino's Pizza, which operates in India through Jubilant FoodWorks, recently opened its 500th store in the country. India is Domino's fourth-largest overseas market and the chain sells around 70% of the country's home-delivery pizzas. Richard Allison, executive vice-president, Domino's Pizza International, says in an interview that being a leader does not mean an end to the learning process and how the chain entered India at the 'appropriate' time. Excerpts:

What is leadership for you?

A leader is someone who is sure about organizational goals and focus, someone who can instantly infuse 'go, get and achieve spirit'. He is someone who provides the required resources to teammates and boosts their motivational levels. A leader is one who is ready to share his formulas, learnings and tricks. He should not be insecure about his own success and position.

Who is your inspiration?

For every person, the first dose of inspiration always comes from parents. I have seen my parents working tirelessly to afford my education and then, Patrick Doyle, Dominos Global CEO, who transformed Domino's business in the US fabulously. I aspire to be hardworking like my parents and a leader like him. Moreover, never underestimate freshers—young enthusiastic freshers infuse phenomenal energy and inspire me a lot.

How do you handle the bad economic scenario, especially when your performance is been constantly watched?

I try to teach my team to focus on priorities. Good and bad economy is a part of business and those who keep their focus on objectives feel confident while answering watchers. No matter what the policy and economic equation is, the fundamentals of team spirit, assurance of job security and right leadership lessons will make you win.

What is the best leadership decision that you have taken so far?

There have been many but one of them was to enter India at the time when it was 'looking' like an exciting market. We grabbed the opportunity at the right time and today, we are aggressively growing in the most exciting market. Today, India is Domino's fourth-largest overseas market after the US, UK and Mexico. Leaders are those who have the intuition of doing things at the best time.

And your worst decision as a leader?

I don't regret decisions, rather I learn and move forward.

Are you open to criticism about your decision in front of your team?

Completely, even I ask my team to suggest what better could be done and what probably went wrong. Being a leader doesn't mean an end to the learning process. Sometimes, your team feels good when you compliment them by saying, 'Oh, I did not knew this, thanks for telling me.' Good lessons are based on bad experiences and I never hide my sour incidents or hard-earned lessons.

How does a leader keeps himself grounded?

It is one of the most important traits a leader should carry. Success should not affect the attitude of a person. The world remembers those who remain grounded, humble throughout and not those who were just good professionals. In the leader-making process, a man turns into a good human being first and a good leader later on.

Can leadership be learnt? How can a manager become a leader?

It can be learnt, if you have a good leader. A good leader can breed another leader. Bad bosses are insecure about their own positions but leaders will let their managers' bloom, they won't feel insecure when their colleagues perform well. I let my team and teammates work, my work is to review, criticize or appreciate them.

Why is leadership so important today?

Leadership is very important because of the growing competition. An organization will go corrupt if the sole focus is on profitability and business. Leadership is a steering which keeps the firm going in the right direction. After all, the brand identity of a company is based on its morals and culture. This is an era of economic uncertainty; the challenges faced by organizations are much more complex and advanced than they were ten years ago. In times of crisis we need to ensure that we effectively communicate with all stakeholders and employees.

In leadership, do actions count more than words?

Actions do count more at times. For instance, if I will arrive late for a meeting, my action will send a wrong message to my team despite several mails and lectures on the value of discipline. Our actions count a lot more than our words.

What is the role of a leader in a sector like fast food chain services?

The fast food services industry is highly innovative; it is a taste-driven sector. In such a case, you have even more scope, because the job of a leader is to differentiate one's organization from the rest in the industry. When I am in India, I turn Indian, I start thinking and eating the way Indians would enjoy. The flexibility to adapt to multiple tastes and identify the best one for a particular region is embedded in the trait of a leader.

You motivate your colleagues on a daily basis but how do you motivate yourself?

Well, my team, through their display of performance and brilliance in their job motivates me back. The opening of the 500th store in India, excellent financials and selection of partners such as Jubilant FoodWorks motivates me every day. Good results are my motivation.

HIMANI CHANDNA GURTOO

'A leader needs to adapt his ego to the firm's value': DIDIER MICHAUD-DANIEL,

CEO, BUREAU VERITAS

Heading a vertical transportation company, as the president of Otis Elevator, and heading a quality assessment and certification company as the CEO of Bureau Veritas all within a space of three weeks, may be fraught with challenges, says Didier Michaud-Daniel, but it certainly doesn't cause any vertigo, because the job of a leader is to motivate and inspire, not to get into the nitty-gritty. Excerpts from an interview:

As a leader, are you nervous shifting from one industry to another?

I have been in Bureau Veritas (BV) for three weeks. I have been meeting all the people who are going to report to me and I must say it's a great team. There was a BV 2015 plan which was already in place—my job now is to achieve this vision. So I can not say I am nervous, but yes, it's a challenge.

What's the difference in your leadership roles at Otis Elevator and at BV?

Otis is a company which is into manufacturing elevators and escalators. BV is a service company. I have to learn about the products. But when you are used to leading people, you can lead anywhere in the world.

If that is the case, then why do some leaders fail when they shift industries?

I think you need to adapt your ego to the values of the firm. If you try to manage a firm or lead with the culture you were in before, you will fail. You can take the good things you learnt in the past but need to adapt your personality to the new company to be accepted by the team because most of the time it's not the issue of the technicality of the job, it's an issue of rejection from the team.

How have you adapted?

I have 100 days of induction which has started already. I was in Shanghai last week, I visited shipyards as I was not familiar with the marine vertical.

But if there was a disagreement between you and a domain expert at BV, as a leader, what would you do?

I would apply my common sense. The people who are working for me are extremely professional—my job is not to do their job. My job is to lead them and achieve an objective. My job is to motivate the employees.

So how would you describe your leadership traits?

It's respect for people, first before anything else. I am direct and transparent—which means that people know quickly what I feel and what I want to achieve. It's quite a simple type of leadership.

You say you are direct—so does that mean you are blunt and don't sugar-coat your critical reviews?

No, when I think I can do something softly but honestly, I say it. If I think something should be improved, I try to tell the people, but keeping their cultural sensitivities in mind.

How do you deal with non-performers?

Most of the time I have met people who are performing. When you explain to the people what you expect from them, they do it. So very rarely did I have an issue about performance. When you are a leader you have to assess people quickly and to understand who could do what. Give them the job where they will perform and also enjoy their job. You need to have passion for your job.

You have also undergone a management course at INSEAD—so can leadership be taught, or is it ingrained in a person?

I think it's ingrained. You can improve it by going to INSEAD for instance, because what you improve is clearly not your leadership style but your knowledge about various things that you need to know when you are a leader.

Are you saying everybody can't be a leader?

No, I didn't say that. I think everyone can be a leader—it depends of course on the circumstances of your life.

TEJEESH N.S. BEHL

'Right now there is a huge leadership vacuum': VINITA BALI,

MANAGING DIRECTOR, BRITANNIA INDUSTRIES

For Vinita Bali, one of India's popular business figures, leadership is about pursuit of excellence, which eventually helps achieve success. Bali, incharge of Britannia, believes that besides other things leadership is foremost about ownership and accountability. In a freewheeling chat, she revealed various facets of leadership.

Is leadership ingrained or can it be nurtured?

It's not just embedded in one to be a leader. Leadership is fairly multidimensional where it's a question of one's own initiatives, the experiences and the context of those experiences. A part of it is contextual and a part of it is an innate desire to do something different and meaningful. For me, leadership is about taking responsibility to change something for the better. It could be an ideology, a product, and a cause for the country or the environment. But yes, all leaders display great courage and responsibility.

Do you think we have nurtured enough leaders after Independence?

We certainly have leaders who have shown leadership skills in different and difficult circumstances. Leadership is not a flash in the pan, or about being opportunistic. It is about consistency. It's a marathon and not a sprint. If you look at some of the emerging industries such as software or biotechnology; all of which is less than 20–25 years old. If you look at the art, or even Hindi cinema; the way themes have changed are all brought about by people who have had enough of status quo.

So, do we have enough leaders…?

Right now there is a huge leadership vacuum. As a country we are continuing to struggle to emerge as an effective democracy. We have to learn to prioritize on what is more important. Also, in many ways it is tougher to be a leader because you have got many more and multiple agendas to cater to. Over a period of time we are dealing with both greater complexity and ambiguity. Thus, the leadership skills themselves have to be very different. It is not about looking up to a leader. We are learning to deal with how do you have conflicting agendas and yet make progress.

You made an unconventional choice early in your career when you chose to work in markets such as Nigeria and South Africa. What was the core reason behind this?

In the 80s, it was quite unusual for somebody from India to go and work in the marketing. Nigeria was an unconventional choice but to my mind it was an opportunity to go and really make a difference. The attraction was to walk into an unfamiliar territory and do something about it. That worked really well, leading to a second opportunity in South Africa in 1994.

Any particular lessons that you picked from making this choice?

When you are thrown into an environment you are not familiar with, the learning ability increases. You become more adaptable and you learn how to establish credibility in a shorter span of time. Also, I have developed another hypothesis that it's easier to bring about a change if you are an outsider. So, if you look at it from a macro perspective the biggest change agent before Independence was Mahatma Gandhi, who more or less was an NRI. He did not have the baggage of the context and reality.

What are your core leadership traits and has it evolved over the years?

I don't shy away from taking ownership and accountability. All leaders must have large amounts of energy and enthusiasm, especially when you are looking at creating a large change. Leaders pursue excellence that leads to success. Pursuit of excellence is inspirational and I see it in sportsmen and in artists. I wish there was a greater pursuit of excellence in the corporate world.

Who do you look up to?

Nelson Mandela and Aung San Suu Kyi are two leaders I admire. They stood for principles and emerged with no semblance of any deterrence after years of isolation. Then there are other sources of inspirations including Steve Jobs and Richard Branson who created and did things differently.

Do you think leadership comes easy to a woman?

Leadership is genderless. Either you have the qualities of a leader or you don't. Leadership is timeless.

RACHIT VATS

'I do not get involved on a daily basis': HARSH GOENKA,

CHAIRMAN, RPG GROUP

Harsh Goenka, who took over as chairman of his family-run RPG group in his early 30s, is now spearheading its global expansion. The Rs 15,000 crore group with interests in tyre, software, power infrastructure and plantations is in a transition phase towards becoming a 'task-oriented tough group to work in,' says Goenka in an interview. Excerpts:

How do you view your role as a leader of a diversified group?

As the chairman of the group, my responsibility is to define the core values of the group and see that we do not deviate from those values. There are sometimes difficult choices to make. I was recently accosted by a competent manager. He did not adhere to the values of the group. If the manager is incompetent and does not adhere to our values, the answer is easy. But if he's competent and still does not adhere to the values, I have come to the conclusion that he should not be with the group.

What is your style of leadership?

My style of leadership is a soft touch non-threatening, non-controlling, directional leadership. I leave my colleagues alone. I have a review mechanism—business review meetings typically once in two months for an entire day—where I engage in critical decision-making. Otherwise if there is something critical where my intervention is needed, I get involved. I do not get involved on a day-to-day basis.

Can you recall an instance where your intervention was required?

Some years ago, in our financial services company, we had unbridled growth. We had built a large portfolio of customers that was not robust. In fact, we took a lot of wrong decisions based on the information that was placed before us, which we took at face value. Somehow, I trusted the team a lot and one fine day realized that the company was near collapse. It did create a lot of losses for the group and in hindsight, I believe I should have gone deeper into the rationale of the decisions and not taken decisions based on figures that were presented to me.

Was there an instance where you felt vindicated by your own decision?

Around 2007–2008 we started building our organization for the future. It also happened to be a time of great uncertainty globally and India was somewhat successful in remaining unaffected, particularly in the manufacturing sector. The easy and more obvious choice would have been to develop an India-centric strategy. But I took the decision to globalize our operations. As a result we expanded geographically and also began acquiring companies. Given the economic scenario, we were able to do the deals at favourable valuations. In hindsight, I believe the decision to think global at that time of uncertainty paid off. Now over 40% of our revenues come from global businesses and we are well on track towards achieving our objective of garnering 50% of our revenue from international operations.

Your son Anant Goenka has now taken over as the managing director of the group's flagship company Ceat. Is it fair to assume he will succeed you as group chairman?

He has a chance as much as anybody else. Merit is the foremost priority. Perhaps, he may have the first chance if all things are equal but the seat is not necessarily his.

Do top executives feel their growth prospect is limited in the promoter-run family set up?

The freedom you have in RPG is much greater than many other workplaces. The freedom you have in Indian business groups are greater than MNCs. Look at the Tatas, the Aditya Birla Group, the freedom that senior managers get is tremendous. You will find this in most business groups, which are not first-generation entrepreneurs. Most second or third-generation business groups have evolved in terms of their management practice and style.

Who inspires you as a leader?

I have no role model. But among several people who inspire me, if it is strategic vision, it is Dhirubhai Ambani. If it is ethics and values, it is J.R.D. Tata or Ratan Tata. If you look at the globalization strategy, something which we are now working very seriously on, it is Aditya Birla because he started the globalization wave.

Is it easy for chairmen who belong to business dynasties to run businesses?

It depends on the person. But yes, in the Indian context people are more obedient to a so-called master, may be the mindset comes from being ruled by the British. People tend to be more loyal to promoters. But again…if a manager finds me not fair and transparent, he may look outside.

MANU P. TOMS AND RACHIT VATS

'A leader needs to anticipate changes': CHANDA KOCHHAR,

MD AND CEO, ICICI BANK

A leader's job, says Chanda Kochhar, MD and CEO, ICICI Bank, is to be a step ahead of competition by thinking ahead of the game, even as she herself gets down to the task of giving shape to her legacy—propel the bank into the league of the world's top 20 banks by size—within her tenure. Excerpts from an interview:

What is the role of a leader in a process driven sector like financial services?

Financial services industry is process-oriented and it doesn't lack innovation. In such a case, you have even more scope, because the job of a leader is to differentiate one's organization from the rest in the same industry.

So how have you differentiated your organization from your competitors?

If you track ICICI's history and look at it currently, you will see that we have always said that the organization should remain ahead of the curve in terms of anticipating the change in the environment and being ready for the change. So as a leader I would look at the next set of changes that are likely to happen and set a vision and a direction for the organization in the context of that environment that is likely to emerge, and not just the environment that is prevailing.

What is the next big game changer that you envision as a leader, to set ICICI Bank apart from the competition?

We are focusing currently on setting up a very sustainable, profitable model of growth. For ICICI, it is partly a game changer because after reaching the scale and size if we set the company on a sustainable and profitable model, it can have a huge multiplier effect on the profitability of the company.

How have you implemented the learning from your mentor KV Kamath in your own style of leadership?

I think as any leader evolves, he/she absorbs a lot from mentors and the persons he/she works with and what emerges finally is his or her own style of leadership. I would say in my style of leadership, I have learnt from my mentors, but it would be difficult to say what part is learnt and what part is my own.

What is your leadership philosophy?

I believe a leader really sets the direction and vision for the organization and then aligns his/her team to move on that path. So in that sense what is actually required of a leader is a balance between vision and execution, dreaming and at the same time being close to reality. You keep looking at the big picture, prepare your organization for that big picture but as you do that, two things become very important—one is that your team has to be fully aligned to move in that direction, and secondly, as you keep moving, you have to keep coming back to reality and keep doing a reality check to see if the direction is correct.

Any examples of course corrections from your own career?

In hindsight, we probably grew our unsecured retail loan business much faster than the ability of the market to absorb that growth. We expected the market to evolve in a certain manner in terms of the credit culture of the individual, growth in the credit scoring models etc., which actually did not happen. In the bargain, our growth was much larger than it was warranted. The way we corrected the course was by actually cutting down the size of the unsecured retail loan business, which in fact meant that for one year, in total terms, our loans and advances actually decreased by 17%. Forget growing in a year, we actually cut back our balance sheet. So it was not an easy decision at all—it was a tough decision.

How do you motivate yourself as a leader everyday?

Well, as I always say, what will give me the biggest high is if we are in the global top 20.

Within the next 10 years?

It has to be much less than that actually.

Within your own tenure?

Yes, of course.

So that's what drives you?

Yes.

TEJEESH N.S. BEHL

'I am much less autocratic now': ADI GODREJ,

CHAIRMAN, GODREJ GROUP

The 69-year-old Godrej Group patriarch, Adi Godrej says leadership is certainly no popularity contest. Good leaders, he says, even when they take decisions not liked by all, owe it to their subordinates to explain the rationale for such decisions. Excerpts from an interview:

What's your leadership style?

I don't want to comment on my leadership style but I will tell what leadership is to me. It's about doing the tough things. One must have a clear vision of the future and work to see how it can be achieved and how your people can contribute to achieve that vision.

So does a leader needs to be ruthless?

I won't like to use the word ruthlessness. One has to be clear that one can't pander on every opinion. One has to keep in mind the long-term interest of the organization. Tough decisions are needed to be taken sometimes and that is the major distinguishing points of good leaders.

So does a leader have to be a loner?

No, but neither does he have to be popular. You must be respected by your staff. Tough decisions can also be respected. Communication is very important. If a leader just makes a one-line announcement that is not a good thing. They must explain what it is.

Any instances of tough decisions you have taken in your life?

There are many. For example, in our joint-ventures (JVs), some years work very well when the interest of both the parties are being met, but after a while, there is not much to learn from each other. In that situation, it is better to be frank and clear that a restructuring is the best way forward and one must be open about it and get it done.

Has your leadership style changed since the time you joined the group?

Oh, there has been a lot of change. I am much less autocratic now. I have become a better listener than what I used to be when I was younger. Things are very different today than when I first joined the group. Leadership styles and dimensions must change with times.

Your children are active in the group. Do they seek any advice from you?

Well, they give me more advice! But I think all three are very passionate and they are very good communicators. Often I find their advice appropriate.

Do you think you have been able to create leaders in your organization?

Well, we have a good succession planning process in our organization and over the years in each of our verticals we have had better leaders to head the business.

Has your succession plan been charted?

As far as my succession is concerned I don't want to comment on that. It is not for public consumption.

But can a non-Godrej surname holder become the group chairman?

As of now our plan is that the chairman of the group and the chairman of various group companies shall be from the Godrej family.

Is hands-on training necessary to become a good leader?

All our family members joined as management trainees. Then they rose in the organization. I think hands-on is absolutely necessary.

Did you also start that way?

No, because at that time our business was much smaller and I started taking leadership decisions at a very young age because I was the first management graduate to join the business.

Who do you draw your inspiration from?

I have great admiration for leadership that was passed down in ancient Greece. So Socrates was Plato's teacher and mentor. Plato was Aristotle's and Aristotle was Alexander's. That is a leadership transfer that I have always admired. Other leaders that I admire are Nelson Mandela, who enabled South Africa to become the most successful African country; I admire Margaret Thatcher as she took some difficult decisions in a socialist Britain which was not doing well economically.

Which particular trait has been common between all these leaders that you have mentioned?

The common factor in good leaders is wisdom. You do not have to be the most intelligent person in the world but I think wisdom is very important to choose to do the right thing.

SACHIN DAVE AND TEJEESH N.S. BEHL

'Every crisis presents an opportunity for a true leader': HARKIRAT SINGH,

MANAGING DIRECTOR, WOODLAND

Leading footwear and apparel brand Woodland was started in Quebec, Canada, as a maker of winter boots, and was launched in India in 1992. The company's managing director Harkirat Singh spoke on a range of issues on leadership in an interview. Excerpts:

How do you define a leader? What are the most important traits of a leader?

A leader is the chief custodian of the brand force of the organization —someone who is sure about organizational goals and focus, and can instantly infuse a 'go, get and achieve' spirit. Passionate curiosity, an inquisitive mind, a simple mindset, the ability to take a complicated situation and boil it down to manageable tasks are all important qualities of a forward thinking leader.

Can leadership be learnt? In other words, how can a manager become a leader?

Yes, leadership is a performance art that one learns. An attitude of leadership can be cultivated by anyone by recognizing the weaknesses in his area of work and then making improvements to overcome them. Simply put, critique your performance, get feedback and keep getting better.

What is the role of a professional leader in a promoter-driven company?

My role is to provide periodic guidance and knock down obstacles in their way. Within the company, people have been promoted and treated on merit. That explains the zero attrition rate among senior professionals at Woodland.

What is the role of a leader in times of a slowdown?

I think it is only in such times that you can differentiate a good leader from an average one. Every crisis presents an opportunity and a good leader is excited by it.

How important is the role of communication in leadership?

Good communication not only helps to lead effectively, but it also helps to lead ethically. By understanding the process and the role of communication, as well as the channels through which communication flows, leaders can increase their effectiveness and accomplish their objectives more optimally.

Can you share some of your experiences during your career where you may have been called upon to take decisions on retrenchment and downsizing?

I try to be fully involved in the hiring process, especially for middle and senior management roles. We have always tried to keep a lean organizational structure which can sustain the market high and lows, while delivering efficiently on the key parameters. Personally, I believe that the real cost of layoffs is much more when viewed in the long-term. Not only does the employees' morale take a hit, but the company also sees a downward spiral, since a lot of factors are at play when employees are laid-off.

What has been the biggest leadership challenge you've faced?

Embracing change, and convincing stakeholders that it is good for them when the company sometimes asks them to come out of their comfort zones. The hard part is all of us react differently to change and that's where leadership comes to play. We have to do the right thing but the hardest time in any transformation is when the results haven't arrived and no one knows exactly when they will. Doing it the slow way, organically, can set us back—while any missteps can translate into expensive mistakes.

Who are the leaders who have inspired you?

There are many CEOs and leaders whom I admire. If I had to pick one, it would be Jack Welch. He has the aggression to win, together with integrity. I also admire Bill Gates. Steve Jobs is another leader whom I admire for his sheer creativity and his refusal to accept mediocrity.

What is the worst decision you have taken as a leader?

Decision making is easy, but good decision making isn't. Also, making the unpopular but right decision is much harder than choosing an alternative that people will find more acceptable.

What is the best decision that you have taken as a leader?

There have been many but one of them was to enter India at the time when it was 'looking' like an exciting market. We grabbed the opportunity at the right time and today, we are aggressively growing in the most exciting market in the world.

What is the biggest leadership lesson that you have learnt?

The best way to make a 'defining-moment' decision is to study all the facts, learn everything you can about the circumstances you're in, evaluate all the pros and cons, undertake a thorough cost-benefit analysis, and then make your decision. It's really got to be well thought out.

What is your leadership mantra?

Be open, be transparent and be authentic.

GAURAV CHOUDHURY

'Leaders are born, not made by education': BALKRISHAN GOENKA,

CHAIRMAN, WELSPUN GROUP

Hailing from the Marwari community that has its origins in Rajasthan, Balkrishan Goenka, chairman, Welspun Group, believes that home-grown lessons—gleaned from everyday conversations in the family—do not necessarily translate into leadership skills in business, as those are some things one can only be born with, and not acquired. Excerpts from an interview:

Marwaris and business always seem to go hand-in-hand— what's the connection?

For Marwaris, business is in their blood, it is in the DNA. This is true as 90% of the families are in business. You live in a business environment all your life. Since childhood, you see your father, grandfather, talking about business most of the time. You get maximum values and learning from your family and friends.

Your mind is tuned to do business and generation to generation it goes on.

So, what's the most valuable lesson you have learnt?

One of my elders told me when I was nine, you have to be in the top three in whatever you do. If you are fourth or fifth, you will be considered an 'also-ran', and it's not worth the effort. So, we like to be among top three in every business we do.

Did your education help you acquire leadership skills?

I believe leading is a natural instinct. You are a born leader. You cannot make someone a leader by education and cannot change certain character traits. A leader should be bold and be able to take decisions, for which one needs to have guts. In a family, all four brothers cannot be a leader.

So if leadership can't be taught, does that mean B-schools are a waste of money? What does MBA give?

MBA is one course which gives you a 360 degree perspective about business. MBA is a big help. Given a chance, I myself would like to do it. But that doesn't mean that it is the only way to succeed. It's not necessary to have an MBA. I think one should have common sense, which is more important.

Who do you think has more common sense—MBAs or non-MBAs?

Well, in my experience, non-MBAs have demonstrated more common sense, but that doesn't discount the value of an MBA degree and in fact, most of our new recruits are MBAs.

The perception about Marwari businessmen is that they are control freaks and don't empower their executives. Would you agree?

When you start something, your leadership style will be more directive. But when you diversify and have multiple businesses, your style will become participatory. It is more of participatory in today's time.

So as a leader, have you learnt to let go?

Leadership is all about extracting the best out of the people you work with. You have to give a lot of power down the line. You cannot be a leader if you want to do everything yourself. All the credit should go down the line and all the blame should rest with the management. It is very easy to blame others. But if there is any failure, it is the management's responsibility. It is a natural leadership style for me. If you cannot build a team but still tell them 'this is your baby', you cannot grow. We have leaders who have grown within the company. Giving power to people, trusting someone, it all involves risk and a leader needs to take that risk.

Which means that some risks would have backfired—any notable mistakes that you can instantly recall?

Plenty. When we started with textiles, we decided we should not only manufacture, but market and distribute our products as well. We wanted to be an end-to-end player. We made Welspun a global brand, we built facilities in the UK, Germany, Portugal, Mexico and started retail in India in a big way. After four years of struggle, we realized it was a mistake on our part. On one hand, we wanted to manufacture and on the other hand, we wanted to be a retailer as well. A retailer can buy only whatever is in demand, leaving your capacity as a manufacturer lying idle. You cannot have two things together. It was a mistake and we corrected it. We sold our Portugal and Mexico units and cut down production in the UK. We reduced our retail outlets to 50 from 300 in India. We were pouring money at the front-end while our capacity wasn't getting utilized at the back-end. We learned from our mistakes, corrected it, booked the losses and moved on.

MANU P. TOMS AND TEJEESH N.S. BEHL

'Leadership style has to be situational': HUBERT JOLY,

PRESIDENT AND CEO, CARLSON REZIDOR HOTEL GROUP

Heading a workforce of 1,70,000 at a $38 Billion hospitality chain is no easy job. Especially, if the chain operates more than a thousand hotels under the Radisson brand and almost the same number of restaurants under TGI Friday's, besides travel service company Carlson Wagonlit Travels, it requires not just deft leadership skills, but plain speaking as well, says Hubert Joly, president and CEO, Carlson Rezidor Hotel Group in an interview. Excerpts:

What are the main attributes of a leader?

First is the ability to set directions. Second is to build a high-performance team depending on circumstances. Third is integrity —doing what is right and essential. And the fourth is producing or delivering quality results.

As a rank outsider to the hospitality industry, do you think the leadership skills required here are different?

Yes and no. Yes, because if you look at various industries such as semi conductors or jet engines, the success factors are very different. For example, R&D would be a very long-term perspective in jet engines and you may need to take a 30-year perspective. So each sector is unique. And no, because the basic leadership attributes tend to always remain the same.

Does your leadership style differ according to geography?

Leadership style has to be situational. One has to deal with different cultures, which have some specificity, though I do believe that human values around the world are actually quite common.

Talking of human values, do you think as far as leaders are concerned morals have changed over time?

The fundamental values of wisdom such as what is the meaning of life, why we are here and what is the purpose of what we do, have been around for a long time. As companies or as individuals we go wrong only when we deviate from these values and the system. The recent crisis is an example of this, when greed becomes pervasive and there is loss of the sense of purpose.

Tell us about your experience as a French man running an American legacy firm?

When I became the CEO of Carlson, it was the fourth time I was moving to the US—we have lived in California twice and in New York twice. Over the years, I have tried to develop a sensitivity to some of the nuances that do not exist particularly in France. For example, in France there is heavy emphasis on theory whereas there is more pragmatism in the US.

What about India?

There is one thing that is very striking in India, which is the difficulty to say no. If you ask somebody to do something, it's very difficult for them to say no.

As a leader, are you a consensus builder or a top-down guy?

I use different styles. Sometimes my style is effective and sometimes it is not.

How do you get rid of non-performers?

The key element of leadership is the development of a high performance team. When you take up the job of a CEO of different companies, you always find great performers, medium performers and bottom performers. If you do not pay attention to this bottom, they drag everybody down. So I never hesitate to remove the bottom performers in terms of their performance or attitudes. It is extraordinary how it uplifts the rest of the group. Now that you have removed the bottom quarter or the bottom third there is a new bottom quarter and bottom third. So it's a constant engineering of the team. Today, in Carlson's global executive team, 70% of the members are new compared to four years ago.

Name two non-business leaders you admire ?

I have great admiration for Winston Churchill, I admire him for his creativity and leadership. In your country, Mahatma Gandhi was somebody extraordinary. As Roosevelt (US President Franklin Delano) said: 'You must do things that you think you cannot do to become a leader. As leaders, we need to do things we have not done before.'

SACHIN DAVE AND TEJEESH N.S .BEHL

'A leader must be quick on his feet': SUNIL GODHWANI,

CHAIRMAN AND MD, RELIGARE ENTERPRISES

Sunil Godhwani, chairman and managing director, has been the driving force behind Religare Enterprises, transforming the firm from a mono line broking-led business to a one-stop shop financial services major offering insurance, wealth management, mutual fund, and loans to small firms. Under his leadership, Religare has seen its revenues climb tenfold in the last five years to nearly Rs 3,200 crore in 2011–12. Godhwani believes that a true leader must have the humility to accept and change a wrong decision. Excerpts from an interview:

What are the key leadership qualities one needs to build in an organization?

A leader must have clarity and vision and have the passion and perseverance to back that vision. A leader should also have the ability to pick the right talent so that the team he/she builds is able to successfully execute the vision. Above all, a leader needs to be quick on his feet in these uncertain times and must have the humility to accept and change wrong or incorrect decisions, if any.

What is the best leadership decision that you have taken so far —listing the company or diversification?

Both in their own right have been decisions that have contributed to the growth and success of the Religare Franchise. The listing of the holding company Religare Enterprises Ltd (REL) way back in 2007 met with good success with the initial public offering (IPO) being oversubscribed a record 161 times. That is a history of sorts. It was also a true recognition of our model by the external world early in our evolution. What followed in a planned manner was then the diversification from a largely mono line broking-led business to a multi asset integrated financial services group.

What is your vision for the group?

At Religare, we are committed to our vision of creating a superlative platform for all our stakeholders namely customers, employees and shareholders, and build an all-encompassing one-stop shop for integrated financial services. Banking is clearly on our radar. If it happens, well and good. But if it doesn't, we will continue to focus and build on what we are doing currently.

What is your leadership mantra?

Develop a deep and wide management team that is completely aligned with your vision and goals. A team that is highly motivated, empowered and happy doing what they are doing, is a team that will be able to deliver seamlessly. One should focus on helping them and enabling them to be successful and they will in turn help the organization succeed. Most importantly, it is very critical to create a culture of teamwork and not that of 'individual heroes'.

Can leadership be taught?

As they say, leaders are often born and not made. Having said that, we have to create the right environment for leaders to be made and grown. Education, grooming and training play a vital role in honing certain skills already exhibited by leaders or a potential leader. We as leaders should have the skills to spot and identify 'tomorrow's leaders'.

As a leader, are you consensus builder?

While my primary objective is to set goals and direction for my company, I believe it is necessary to build a consensus. When we debate about a particular move, we very clearly know the merits and demerits of that decision and its likely implications. When we discuss it threadbare, we get opinion of other leaders on board. To that extent, delivery of that objective or the action needed to start a process becomes easier.

Name the two non-business leaders you admire the most?

Nelson Mandela and Mother Teresa.

Since September 2008, the world has fallen into a maelstrom of serial crises. What is the role of a leader in these times?

One of the reasons why the world fell into this maelstrom is that a small minority of heads of companies thought they were great leaders and got carried away. This made them far removed from ground realities. One can get into such a situation, when people close themselves from the dynamics of a the real world, which is evolving constantly. It is absolutely essential for a leader to be conscious of such situations, for you would never realize when you have fallen of the cliff.

Leaders have to often carry the cross of other's wrong doings and inefficiencies, the global banking sector today, for instance. What role can good leadership play to counterbalance this image?

I do not agree with such generalizations. Leadership, in the final analysis, is a very individual trait. If we look across history and also the contemporary world, there are certain individuals who stand out in each sector as universally acknowledged leaders.

GAURAV CHOUDHURY

'If you are not listening, you will miss the bus': NAINA LAL KIDWAI,

GROUP GM AND COUNTRY HEAD, HSBC INDIA

Naina Lal Kidwai, group general manager and country head, HSBC India, spoke on issues ranging from the importance of values, the need for a consultative approach and the role of intuition in decision making. Excerpts from an interview:

How difficult is it to lead a foreign bank at a time when the banking industry all over the world is going through some uncertainty?

We have to learn to live in uncertain times. It is all about volatility today. But you require the same skills that you required in the early 2000s to able to steer through. It is flexibility and having a strategy in place but what is critical today is to review constantly. You need to keep continuously reviewing and redefining those strategies while keeping your eyes and ears open. You also need to be aware of competition.

How do you manage to drive your employees to perform especially when your bank is looking at slashing jobs?

It is realignment and not downsizing—realignment because of upgradation of technology and people do understand that. There have been changes in the sizes of different teams and there is a requirement to have fewer and better.

Is it difficult for leaders to motivate employees when there is uncertainty about jobs and increments?

Let's be honest. There is dead weight everywhere and companies decide what is dead weight and here are people today who do not have a full day's work, so it is important that those people are willing to move to new areas or places and often they are unwilling, and companies are left with little choice. Your skill set needs to be constantly enhanced and often people do not want that. In any organization priorities change, products change and you need to move with that. But yes, morale does suffer if you suddenly see your friend not there anymore and I am sure there are cases where people who need not have gone have had to go, but again those who are in the organization must sustain and have patience and understanding of the situation. At the same time, organizations must reassure people that they are not on the list and such an exercise does not happen again and again, and that they must now focus on work. I feel if organizations have to resort to downsizing, they should do it in one go so that there is no apprehension or fear among the employees who are still there.

What is the mantra of success?

Besides being open and flexible you need to have a consultative approach, though it cannot be a committee based decision-making process. When my senior management meets, we do have disagreements. I would be worried if everybody agreed, there should be some disagreements. I challenge everybody and I need to be convinced but I am the first to accept if I am wrong, but again only if I am convinced. The way we disagree must be constructive.

What do you do if there is no emergence of one voice and as a leader you need to take a quick decision?

When disagreements become ugly, a CEO's role comes into play. Let me tell you when my top team is not in agreement, I have often taken decisions intuitively. Somehow, intuitively you know it is the right decision.

How often have you taken decisions based on just intuitions?

Almost all the time. Intuition gets honed with experience. Today, I can rely on my intuition. Intuition laced with experience is the key.

What is critical to leadership?

Values. Building values is the key and you need to choose the right people and train them. You need to be open and ready to listen to your people. If you are too centralized, if you are not listening, you will miss the bus, you need to be closely in touch especially where your customers are interfacing and like I said, you should be aware of competition.

Is it difficult to be a woman leader in India compared to the Western world?

I don't think so. In India, it is much easier for a woman to be a leader because of the social and family set up—family and children are taken care of. You don't need to bother about them whereas the case is not the same in the West. I have seen women finding it much more difficult to juggle between the two and managing both ends is naturally a lot difficult there, they have to practically do everything on their own and that is tough.

MAHUA VENKATESH

'A leader needs to lead by example': S.D. SHIBULAL,

CEO AND MD, INFOSYS

Leading from the front and leading by example is what sets a leader apart from his followers, which is why leaders need to be self-disciplined, transparent and objective according to S.D. Shibulal, chief executive officer and managing director, Infosys. Excerpts from an interview:

What is the role of a leader in a company such as Infosys with experienced divisional heads who have clear cut goals to follow?

It is the leader's responsibility to raise aspirations, create hopes, deliver performance, drive transformation and lead from the front. It is true for Infosys and for any other organization. I don't believe that organizations can run on an auto-pilot mode. For instance, when Infosys talks about aspiring for the next generation consulting and technology corporation it is my responsibility to raise and create that aspiration for all stakeholders such as clients, employees or investors. Further, during the challenging times when there are uncertainties, doubts and lack of confidence the leader has to create hope. Leadership is about delivering performance and a leader needs to lead by example.

So what role do you see for yourself in steering the company at a time when there are talks of double dip recession in the global economy?

This is not the first time when Infosys is witness to a tough external environment. Similar challenges were present when Kris (current executive co-chairman of Infosys, S Gopalakrishnan) took over. Yet he ran the company well. So, I should take decisions and run the corporation. It all depends on a couple of things. Number one is the strategic direction we are taking; we are aspiring to be the next generation consulting and technological firm in the next five to seven years. So that is an important component of all the decision making that I need to do. Second is the leadership performance that I want to continue. There has been a legacy of good performers and I wish to continue with that. Third is the environment in which we operate. Fourth is the style in which I will operate. I believe that if you can run a company 'good' in good times then you can run it 'better' in bad times.

But then how do you deal with laggards, people who can not deliver?

As I said a leader's role is to drive performance and to manage performance over a period of time it needs to be based on data in a transparent manner, merit-based and objective. So as long as you can demonstrate that you have based your decisions on data, based on merit and is transparent, you can take any tough decision.

How do incidents such as the multi-crore Satyam scam, which put the Indian IT industry in a bad light, affect leaders?

When Satyam scam happened I was the COO of Infosys and I did not see any negative impact of it then and I do not see anything now. Clients too saw it as a single and one-off incident. It does create a situation where the clients will ask you a few more questions. But as long as your foundation is right, things sail through. Infosys' foundation is on running the business legally and ethically so the clients see it and move on. It (Satyam scam) was an unfortunate incident.

Let's talk about the big leadership debate—do you believe that a manager can become a leader?

A leader has to be an excellent manager but an excellent manager may not be a good leader. So when we talk about acquiring leadership skills, an excellent manager can acquire those skills and become a leader. An excellent manager can transform into a leader. Though they are two different roles yet there is no reason why one cannot transform from one role into another.

So you feel that leadership qualities can be learnt or are they are inherent in an individual?

All of us are born with certain leadership traits. I cannot think of any individual who does not have any leadership trait. Yes, some may be born with more traits than others, but leadership is something that can be taught and acquired. I believe that many of the leadership capabilities can be acquired.

What should a young professional cultivate in them right from the very beginning if he or she aspires to be a leader one day?

Anyone on this journey should realize that it is a marathon and not a sprint. So discipline in all aspects is an important thing. The most valued commodity in tomorrow's world will be ethics and values. So when I talk about marathon, it covers the fact that it is a long and hard run that requires hard training and it is a transformation most marathon runners practice for ages.

VIVEK SINHA

'A leader listens to, respects others' opinions': ALESSANDRO BENETTON,

CHAIRMAN, BENETTON GROUP

Alessandro Benetton, heir of the Italian clothing and accessories major, the Benetton Group, aims to act like the 'conductor of an orchestra' for the organization, which is trying to make a seamless transition to the second generation. Amid a deepening European crisis, the new chairman is considered tough enough to introduce bold changes in product and strategy to revive the sinking business. The son of Luciano Benetton, founder of the group, Alessandro set up his own private equity firm—active in the private equity field in Italy and France, with assets of over €1.3 billion—before joining the family group. A Harvard alumnus, Alessandro started his career with Goldman Sachs International, as a mergers and acquisitions analyst.

What is leadership for you?

I believe the role of leadership today should be one of guidance. A leader must not only take responsibility for decision-making, but also create organizations in which knowledge is widespread, so people can work together to build value and develop the business.

Who inspires you?

First Luciano, for his driving innovation and far-sightedness. And also the American management guru, Michael Porter, my mentor at Harvard, where I received my MBA education. Good role models are very important, though you have to be able to find your own way in life and have the courage to be yourself.

The euro zone is under pressure, the economy is sinking. How do you handle the bad economic scenario, especially when your performance is constantly being watched?

It's important, in my opinion, to view this period of crisis not least as an opportunity to rethink and improve our system so that we'll be ready and prepared when economic conditions improve. It's at times of discontinuity such as these that companies like ours can reflect on their position and launch a new business direction. It's also true, unfortunately, that society today is used to expecting results in the very short term, whereas generating solutions to more complex organizational issues requires planning and a greater amount of time.

Is there a difference in the style of a leadership for those who manage a family business and for those who lead an organization on a salaried basis?

There may be a difference in the passion for your work, which in the case of a family business, is felt as manifestation of a business culture that you have always been part of. Having roots and traditions is important to help you look at the future and create new chapters in your story.

What is the best leadership decision that you have taken so far?

Only time will tell if a decision was a good one or not. In this regard, I think delisting was a major step for the future of Benetton Group. We decided to delist from the Milan stock exchange to avoid a routine mind-set and realign this aspect, too, to fit the long-term perspective in which we operate.

…And your worst decision?

I wouldn't be a very shrewd leader if I were to admit one…

Being a leader of a giant apparel fashion house, how do you keep yourself updated about fashion around the globe—especially in countries like India with reserved cultures?

Apart from my personal interest, which makes me an attentive observer of trends, I travel around the world to get a sense of the upcoming fashion and lifestyle trends of young people. Life is one of our sources of inspiration, as are the arts, architecture and the web. They are all expressions of an increasingly global, interconnected world with which we have established a solid relationship. Regarding India, during my recent trip there I perceived a great enthusiasm for looking at the future, with far more confidence and energy than ever before.

You are both a Harvard graduate and the heir of a family run business. Do you think leadership runs in one's DNA or can be learnt in MBA institutes?

I think everything is talent, it's partly innate, and the rest is down to learning, commitment and a lot of hard work. And being aware that a day when you learn something new, is a day well spent.

Are you open to debates on your decisions with your co-workers?

Sharing, and respecting others' opinions are fundamental teamwork values. It's important to listen to one's co-workers' comments and opinions. Then, you can decide on your priorities according to your conscience and competence.

What is your leadership mantra?

I think there's more than one. Firstly, leadership consists of the ability to make decisions and shoulder responsibility. Secondly, as I said before, it is also the ability to create organizations that generate ideas and creativity. Then, the capacity to work in a team and making teamwork a vital tool to manage an increasingly complex business world.

HIMANI CHANDNA GURTOO

'Experiment, err, emerge stronger': AJAY S. SHRIRAM,

CHAIRMAN, DCM SHRIRAM CONSOLIDATED

Ajay S. Shriram, chairman and senior MD of DCM Shriram Consolidated Ltd, has been the driver of his company's success story. As the director of the International Fertilizer Industry Association and the vice-president of the Confederation of Indian Industry, he reflects on corporate India's track records. Excerpts from an interview:

Do you find leading a family-owned company more challenging at a time when the craze is to switch to multinationals?

Ours is a professionally-run family company and a leader has to manage people, whether it is in an MNC or elsewhere. The formula cannot be different—you require good people. In fact, being promoters of the company, we have the biggest stake and therefore, we can bring in more passion and genuine feelings, which can be injected into people.

How easy or tough is the decision-making process as you have senior leaders in your team who are not from the family?

For me, decision-making has always been a joint process with my brother Vikram, we always consult each other on almost all issues. That apart, we do have senior people as part of the top management team. And we naturally differ on several issues, but that is just what we want. We do not want a situation of having a yes-man. If that is the case, we might as well have stenographers.

How difficult has it been to steer a company at a time when the economy is slowing down?

When the gun is on your head, you start thinking differently and we have done that in the last one year. Not just slowdown, we were also impacted by non-availability of coal, and naturally we had to experiment with alternative measures. We took it as a personal challenge and since we started experimenting with other sources, coal mines, we could successfully offset 70% of the impact. These measures that we undertook have not only helped us during the crisis but will help us in the future as well.

The employees of your firm have stuck on for decades, especially at an age when staff keep switching jobs. How have you managed that?

We believe we are a humane organization—an organization that has immense concern for its people. We are lenient and often our level of tolerance is a little too much.

Does it affect the firm's performance ?

Maybe it does, but that is what we stand for. We are there with our people and we are tolerant, even if it means that the performance suffers a bit. But by and large, I have seen if you stand by your people, they stand by you. We focus on the issue of commitment. Once we commit, we stand by our word.

What is your guiding mantra?

Our philosophy is that for an organization to function effectively, one needs the right person for the right job at the right time. And, that person needs to be motivated and should have clarity about the future.

As a leader, how do you motivate your employees?

We give a lot of space to our people. It is very important to allow them to grow, allow them to make mistakes. If you don't make mistakes, either you are God or just that you don't take decisions. So, as an employee you must experiment, make mistakes and come out stronger. It is a different case if an employee keeps repeating his/her mistakes, but largely I have seen if you give them space, they come out with their best.

At a time when most companies have reduced increments, how difficult has the situation been for you?

I believe employees should get increments, based on what we think is fair. However, when the business is down, you have to moderate increments and you need to have logic for what you do, you cannot be unfair. There needs to be complete transparency.

Who has influenced you the most?

My parents. They have taught us what's right and what's wrong. Once my father got a photographic enlarger and in those days, it cost him £70. At the airport, when the customs officer asked him the price, he said exactly the amount he paid. The custom officer told him if he disclosed a lower price, he wouldn't have to pay duties. But he refused and paid whatever was due. Such incidents have taught us a lot in life. When we joined the company, we were based in Kota, where our factory is, and we have learnt work even from the workers.

MAHUA VENKATESH

'Biz is more common sense than academics': FRITS VAN PAASSCHEN,

PRESIDENT AND CEO, STARWOODS HOTELS

As the head of a hospitality company straddling nine hospitality brands including Le Meridien, Sheraton and St. Regis, Frits van Paasschen, president and chief executive officer of the $16 billion (Rs 88,000 crore) Starwood Hotels & Resorts Worldwide says that the key component of his leadership style is communication right down the hierarchy. Excerpts from an interview:

How do you define a leader?

We are living in a time when things are changing more quickly than ever before. In such times, leadership is not about managing the status quo, but literally about leading the people to a new place and a new way of operation. As the world becomes more complex, the notion of the 'crowd sourced' strategy of management—having a dialogue directly with associates—is critical.

As a leader, what is the biggest crisis that you have faced?

For most of us the financial crisis of 2008 marks the most dramatic episode that collectively affected us. As a leader, what I learnt from the crisis was the importance of communication and the importance of being clear about what we as a company were doing about the crisis and what the implications of those decisions were. In a business like ours, with a presence in over 100 countries with so many associates, there was almost no way you could communicate too much. The absolute standard about the importance of communication was very high. It tested my ability and the ability of my leadership team.

What are your views on managing leadership transition—one of the biggest challenges of corporations?

From my own perspective, it is important to know the people who report to me. It is also equally important to know the people who report to them, in order to develop a broader perspective. In general, I think succession planning and having a transparent career growth plan with a consistent vocabulary through a uniform performance matrix is critical. I don't think today's business environment requires many managers. It requires more leaders of small units rather than having a monolithic system.

Who are the leaders that have inspired you?

I am a keen student of history and I believe lessons from the past can be very useful. People whom I draw inspiration from include Benjamin Franklin, a statesmen such as Nelson Mandela, and independent European thinkers of the renaissance period. In many respects, I find reading about them is much of an inspiration. I have also benefitted from the mentorship of a large number of people along the way. I think the notion of a self-made man or a woman for that matter is a bit of a myth. We all enjoy the support and mentorship of people along the way. Human resource systems are important, but inspiration and mentorship are equally important.

How important is communication in leadership?

The challenge of leadership boils down to communication. Leadership is about taking people to a new place. You need to read a situation, articulate what that situation is and talk to people about it. Defining a culture, changing a way of doing business and articulating a strategy are fundamental.

What is your leadership mantra?

My mantra is to 'listen first'. A leader should not state his or her point of view unabashedly at the beginning of a discussion. As a leader if you do that, you shut down a conversation. If a leader walks up and says the sky is blue, nobody in the room will be comfortable pointing out that it is untrue as it is night actually. Business is more about common sense rather than academic pursuits. Things are either fairly straightforward or incredibly complex and unpredictable.

GAURAV CHOUDHURY

'A true leader gives people space to work': QIMAT RAI GUPTA,

CHAIRMAN, HAVELLS

Havells India Ltd is a $1.3 billion (Rs 7,000 crore) electrical goods company and a power distribution equipment manufacturer. In 2007, it leapfrogged into the league of the world's top five lighting companies after acquiring Sylvania. Today, Havells owns brands such as Crabtree, Sylvania, Concord, Luminance and Standard. Its former chairman, the late Qimat Rai Gupta had spoken on a range of leadership and management issues. Excerpts from an interview:

What, according to you, are the key traits of a leader?

Leadership is about giving space to people to work, empathizing with them and listening to their issues and suggestions. A leader must be a visionary, he must be motivational, inspirational and acknowledgeable. A leader must be able to build a stronger and effective team and enable them to perform. Finally, you cannot do everything on your own. Integrity and ability to learn are a few more of the key qualities of a leader.

Do you think leadership is an inborn trait or it can also be acquired?

Leadership is a trait that naturally comes to some; it is ingrained in their DNA. That said, leadership skills can be taught as well as acquired. It is a multidimensional trait and one cannot say that only when an individual has 'x' number of qualities can he or she be a leader. Each one of us has some leadership traits and some can be acquired over a period of time. The key to being a successful leader is the ability to learn from various situations that you find yourself in.

What is the biggest leadership lesson that you have learnt?

I am highly influenced by the Srimad Bhagavad Gita. It teaches us how to maintain inner peace while performing the most complex tasks, accept the ups and downs of life with detachment and overcome uncertainty and anxiety about the future with faith in God. These lessons hold true in business as well. I have taken life changing decisions and the Srimad Bhagavad Gita has always been my guide.

How difficult or easy is it to cultivate leaders in a promoter-driven company?

A promoter-driven company brings a certain amount of passion —and that is not bad at all. An organization needs to build leaders and that's the way to grow. My journey so far cannot be completed without different leaders within the company. We disagree on a lot of issues, but that's healthy. That's how we learn, understand and grow better as individuals and as an organization.

As a leader, does competition bother you?

No. I believe competition is healthy for a company to grow and it teaches you to stay a step ahead. It forces you to think creatively and innovate all the time. Everyone has a space to grow, one just needs to respect that.

As the captain of this ship, are you satisfied with the journey so far?

I guess the answer is both yes and no. When I started my journey, did I know that we will come this far? No. So, to that extent, this has been a great journey. But Havells still has a long way to go. To me it seems that the journey has now started. We may be recognized globally today, but we intend to take the company to greater heights. The acquisition of Sylvania was done with this aim in mind.

What is the role of leadership in nurturing relationships with vendors and customers?

It's the duty of the leader to invest in building and strengthening relationships. This is more important in consumer-centric businesses. The only way to nurture relationships is by being truthful, transparent and determined to achieve collective goals. In our company we have built our business with over 5,600 dealers, purely on the basis of trustworthiness, quality, transparency, efficiency and determination to succeed.

What are the key lessons on motivation that you have learnt over the years?

I started my entrepreneurial journey way back in 1958, with virtually no money in my wallet. I did not have a large base for financing a capital investment, but had the ambition, passion and confidence to excel, to make it big. As the company started to grow, I was fortunate enough that I came across the right opportunities at the right time. I have always believed in the power of a brand, and that is why in 1971 when the word 'brand' was unheard of, I invested in buying the brand 'Havells'. It was a very popular, home grown brand amongst the electrical trading community. This was followed by another turning point in my journey—the acquisition of one of the world's leading lighting brand 'Sylvania' in 2007. I am of the view that as an entrepreneur you must believe in yourself, learn to take setbacks in your stride and stay focused on the ultimate goal. At the same time, a leader also needs to build a loyal team of co-workers who will be with him through thick and thin.

GAURAV CHOUDHURY

'A good leader should be a daydreamer': ONKAR S. KANWAR,

CHAIRMAN, APOLLO TYRES

H e is nearing 70, but Onkar S. Kanwar, chairman of Apollo Tyres, is like his company—fitter than ever before. Operating in an industry beset with old technology and archaic business ethos, he has successfully managed to steer the company to the position of India's first global tyre manufacturer, with two overseas acquisitions—South Africa's Dunlop in 2006 and the Dutch Vredestein in 2009. As he says, leaders should lead from the front. Excerpts from an interview:

How do you define a leader?

A good leader has to be a visionary. He should be able to define the vision clearly, strategically and motivate people towards achieving it. He also has to lead from the front. The critical thing is that he should be able to get his people excited about his ideas so that they give their 100%.

What are the three most important traits of a leader?

There are certain basic values that are a must. Top of the list is the ability to communicate directly, efficiently and unambiguously. He also should have basic integrity so that nobody can point fingers at him at any given point of time. Also, he should be transparent and not scheming.

As the head of the Rs 10,000 crore Apollo group, how do you cultivate leaders?

I have always believed that my people are more important than anything else. They are my true assets. One of our greatest success is that we work as a team where goals are shared. We invest in people and make them part of the decision-making process. There is responsibility on them and that makes them leaders in their field.

What is the role of a professional in a promoter-driven company like Apollo?

I am not driving the company. Only overseeing it and conducting board meetings. It is driven by our 16,000 employees across 3 continents and rightly so. Almost 54% of this firm is owned by FIIs and banks, and I am answerable to them. Apollo tyres is not run on the basis of my whims and fancies but thorough professionals who take smart decisions. I always used this chair as a trustee. Within the company, people have been promoted and treated on merit. That explains why the attrition rate among senior professionals at Apollo is zero.

What is the role of a leader at a time when macro-economic indicators are uncertain and growth cannot be taken for granted?

I think it is only in these times that you can differentiate a good leader from an average one. When the going is good then it is relatively easy and everybody is growing. But when times are tough that is when one needs to show courage and innovate. Every crisis presents an opportunity and a good leader is excited by it. We at Apollo are very bullish and it gives us extra motivation to keep growing in a challenging market.

What is more desirable, a charismatic and larger than life leader or a low profile one?

Both are necessary. There has to be a balance. What is more important is that one should be a daydreamer. Dreams in the night are of no use. One should have dreams during the day so that you can think out of the box and act on it. Whether it is with charisma or by quietly working, is irrespective.

SUMANT BANERJI

'Defeat comes only when you give up—and don't bounce back': ATUL SINGH,

PRESIDENT AND CEO, COCA-COLA INDIA

Coca-Cola India has witnessed strong growth for twenty-four consecutive quarters under Atul Singh, the company's president and chief executive officer. In a free wheeling chat, Singh talks about the democratic work culture within the company that allows anyone to discuss and debate business, but at the same time, teaches them to be accountable. Excerpts:

Coca-Cola is a US based firm and a cola drink is primarily an American concept. In this backdrop, how difficult is it to constantly Indianize your brand and other products under its ambit?

Our product portfolio includes a great number of Made in India and Made for India products such as Thums Up, Limca or Maaza that were acquired within India by us over a period of time. We have also created specific products within India like the Minute Maid Nimbu Fresh, essentially a Nimbu Paani, and tweaked others like the Minute Maid Pulpy Orange for the Indian palate. So, we have a mix of both international brands such as Coca-Cola, Sprite and Fanta and brands that are more local. We may be a US firm in terms of origin but we do operate within the local fabric. Across the 200 countries that we operate in, the 'chalta hai' attitude is widely prevalent in India.

When dealing with your business associates how do you instill a competitive attitude in them?

We encourage debates and discussions, through which one can really delve deep into issues, problems and solutions. For instance, when we launch new products, have expansion plans chalked out, or come up with a new strategy, we like a transparent and open environment. We have built a culture where anybody can speak up but whoever works with us in our system is also accountable to someone in the system, be it the brand manager, marketing manager or a franchise manager in a franchise.

You mean there are no restrictions where an individual gets to speak only to their line managers…

Yes, there are absolutely no restrictions. In fact, I have an open door policy. Anyone can come to see me and anyone can email me. And people do this. I have breakfast several times in a year with all the employees. I hold dialogues with our bottling partners, our associates and our trade partners. We encourage discussions and debates.

Coca-Cola being a global company, how difficult is it for you to communicate with senior executives with diverse work cultures?

I have worked across continents for the last 25 years, and I have noticed that people do have similarities. People are different but there are a lot of common factors as well. You learn to adapt your leadership style in a particular situation or a particular environment. For instance, whether I am in China or India, I need to explain the same concept and issues in a slightly different manner so that the people understand it. Similarly, when I am making a presentation to a senior executive from US, I would adapt my style and the message accordingly. But, the message remains the same, it is only the style of delivery that changes every time.

What is the best leadership decision that you have taken so far?

Well, the best decision I took was to come back to India. This was around seven years ago. And, I feel that the core team that I built for the company after my return to India has served as my biggest strength. I have also been able to keep this team motivated in such a way that we have been able to grow our business for twenty-four consecutive quarters—out of which growth in eighteen quarters has been in strong, double digits.

Great, that's impressive. Also, what has been your low point— your worst decision as a leader?

Well, in hindsight, I think some of the changes that we did make could have been implemented a lot faster.

Can you elaborate…?

You know there are times when something is not working out with an individual and you want to make a change but you delay and give the person a little more time, but even then it doesn't work. So, when I look back, it is some of those changes that I should have made a bit faster. You know, there are wartime generals and peacetime generals. There are individuals who do really well when the business is doing well, and then there are individuals who do really well during crisis. But getting the right person to do the right job at the right time is the key. I think we may not have made those decisions as fast as we needed to—and that's something I feel could have been done faster.

How do you tackle defeat?

Well, defeat comes at every stage in you life or your career but you need to bounce back. I will tell you one instance when I was seventeen years old and in school. This was the time when I was in the school's hockey team and we were participating in a hockey tournament. We won every match, went to the finals but lost the match during penalty strokes. And I was one of the players who missed his penalty stroke. For a 17-year-old boy, that was a total disaster. But I made a very minute assessment of my mistakes and this assessment allowed me to bounce back. You know, the journey does not get over if you encounter one defeat or after you have lost one battle. Defeat comes only when you give up and don't bounce back.

VIVEK SINHA

'Give and you shall receive': PATRIZIO DI MARCO,

PRESIDENT AND CEO, GUCCI

Patrizio di Marco, Gucci's president and CEO, wants to be remembered as someone who fine-tuned the positioning of the fashion goods maker—a brand that was already a legend. As someone who believes in the 'give and you shall receive' philosophy, Marco believes that a true leader must empower his people to draw out their best. Excerpts from an interview:

What are the key elements that make a true leader?

To be a true leader you have to have a clear vision and mission. Then, it is important to have great people around you. And if you have great people around you, you have to empower them to do what they are capable of. This means believing in your team and at the same time recognizing that there will always be occasions when mistakes are made. That should not, however, deter you from keeping faith. I also believe it is fundamental that you treat your staff well. It is a 'give and you shall receive' philosophy. You have to train your people to give them an opportunity to perform at their best. This is what a smart leader does in a company.

How easy or difficult is it for a leader to remain one?

It is much more difficult to nurture leadership than to actually become a leader. You have to act in a way that is consistent with your vision, taking into consideration how the world is changing and the directions of these changes, anticipating them even, and creating a legitimate and authentic consensus around you.

How important is it to be nice to people to be a true leader?

If you are a leader, you need to have a clear and transparent relationship with your people, for instance to speak out when things are not going well. You talk with them and take the best decision for the company and for the people. It's not a matter of being nice or impolite, it's a matter of transparency.

Who, according to you, are leaders (you mentioned Domenico de Sole, Yves Carcelle, Patrizio Bertelli)?

All of them have been great mentors for me; from each one of them I have learned something different. You have to always be capable to observe the best in every person you deal with.

Among the top echelons of brand and branding, what is the role that Gucci plays in terms of its leadership?

Glamour, craftsmanship and social responsibility combine in a formula that I believe truly distinguishes Gucci in the international luxury goods sector today, making it authentic, relevant and a leader rather than a follower. Over 90 years have passed since our founder Guccio Gucci established the values that are still the foundations of Gucci's DNA today.

What all changes have you brought into Gucci after taking over as the CEO?

My goal, starting almost four years ago, was basically to bring Gucci back to its roots. The story of a wonderful brand that is definitely about fashion, is definitely cool, is definitely an authority in the fashion world, but a brand that at the same time has a 90-year-old history, which has a real heritage, has products that are truly artisanal and made by hand. The intention is—and was—primarily to stress the great wealth that has always been inside the company, but for a number of reasons, has not been spoken about as it should have been. There is no doubt that Gucci is a legendary brand. But there is also no doubt that the positioning of the brand has been somewhat fluctuating over time. And this is, primarily, because of the many lives that this company has lived. In the last four years, we have moved to fine tune the positioning of the brand. This has been achieved through a rebalancing of the product offer with a greater emphasis on more precious and sophisticated products, by creating a more evident and consistent link between seasons and collections, by focusing the assortment within the collections and reviving the brand's icons such as the Bamboo, Jackie and Stirrup bags and the renowned Gucci Loafer, which celebrates its 60th anniversary in 2013. The brand has established a higher-level positioning and exclusivity, recapturing the more knowledgeable client as it continues to attract aspirational customers.

What has made you a name to reckon with in luxury?

Gucci is a brand that is larger than life, which will outlive all of us. I would like to be remembered as a CEO who fine-tuned the positioning of the Gucci brand.

VINOD NAIR

'A leader inspires people with his knowledge, spirit': K.P. SINGH,

CHAIRMAN, DLF

A majority of successful business leaders, says DLF Chairman K.P. Singh, have a personal stake in the success of their company, which is not just financial but also emotional, though good leaders also need knowledge and charisma. The trailblazing realty tycoon spoke about his leadership style in an interview. Excerpts:

How do you define a leader?

A leader has to be a multifaceted personality with a sound knowledge of his subject. He should be very hard working. You will never find a good leader who is lazy. Three most important traits of a leader are: knowledge and charisma to earn respect, good listener with ability to inspire and motivate people around, and to be a hard-working team builder with a lot of common sense.

As the leader of the DLF Group, how do you cultivate leaders?

The low key but highly effective people that I had in my team were picked up on the merits of their grass-roots connect, since assembling land was a major challenge, and for that I needed people who can communicate and connect well with the farmers. For the rest of the challenges, since it was a very testing time for DLF to cope with all kinds of roadblocks and attacks, I knew I had to be at the helm of affairs myself with a hands-on approach.

Can leadership be learnt? How can a manager become a leader?

Yes, leadership can be learned. It can be in the genes, to some extent, but merely genetic traits have no meaning if it is not harnessed by training. Some of the great political leaders don't necessarily come from political families but they have a great knack of mass connect.

What is the role of a professional leader in a promoter-driven company and how difficult is a transition from one generation to another?

As the head of DLF family, I was aware of the next level of leadership challenge and it is here that I was monitoring my son Rajiv Singh who was shaping up as one of the finest corporate professionals, both in terms of strategy as well as tactical delivery. I always knew of his determination to evolve a new model for DLF's leadership. Time has changed, the style has changed and the requirements have also changed. The term promoter with a negative connotation is a loose term, in my opinion. You call them promoter, but I call them initial investor. They are the one to have an investment, stake, vision and emotional attachment to be passionate about the enterprise. The best companies these days, nine out of 10, I would say are those which are run by promoters who are great professionals. Why Reliance Industries is doing well is because Mukesh Ambani himself is a great professional.

Which leaders have inspired you?

My flair to take people along and learn lessons even from critics was something that rewarded me with the mentorship of two great legends—George Hoddy and Jack Welch. Hoddy taught me a lot about leadership, team work, management and business strategy. Jack Welch instilled in me a burning desire to think big and aim to be number one.

What has been the biggest leadership challenge that you have faced?

I would say the biggest leadership challenge was to convince policy makers to allow private sector to play a proactive role in India's urbanization. Along with this I had to also face the challenge of assembling thousands of acres of land without any legal hassles and mostly without any money.

What is the biggest leadership lesson that you have learnt?

The biggest leadership lesson I have learnt is that a leader is the one who inspires people with his knowledge. One must have the spirit to not give up, something I very strongly believe in and hence my autobiography is also titled *Whatever the Odds.*

GAURAV CHOUDHURY

'A leader takes fast decisions': RAM CHARAN,

BUSINESS GURU

Ram Charan is a highly sought after business advisor, speaker and writer. Famous among senior executives for his uncanny ability to solve their toughest business problems, he is well known for providing advice that is not only down to earth but also takes into account real-world business complexities. He spoke on a range of leadership issues in a interview. Excerpts:

The Indian economy is going through a period of slowdown and uncertainty. What advice would you give to India's leaders?

Top financial administrators in India's finance, commerce and external affairs ministries need to hammer out an efficient system of coordination for effective policy-making that is consistent and is aimed at attracting greater foreign direct investment (FDI). In India, it is important for these three ministries to coordinate more along with active collaboration with the Reserve Bank of India

(RBI). No country can really grow without having FDI, because FDI brings in capabilities. It is important for India's political and economic leaders to make it clear that it is not going to have inconsistent policies. A lot of questions were raised about India's policies in board rooms of foreign companies after the government had announced a proposal to impose retroactive taxes (on corporate mergers and acquisitions). Leaders should realise such moves cause a lot of harm to a nation's image.

What are the challenges that leaders face in the current period of economic uncertainty?

Turbulent times have been here before. Leaders in business, government and politics have faced this before. There is nothing new about the challenges that leadership faces. But there are some things that are different. The size of the world economy is $70 trillion and, despite the slowdown, it is expected to grow at 3% per annum, adding about $2 trillion. The bigger question to ask is: Who is getting a greater share of that $2 trillion?

What are the causes of the current turbulence?

It is important to first know the causes of turbulence. It is absolutely critical to realize that less than 100 leaders in the world of finance have caused this meltdown and instability in the global financial system. Alan Greenspan, the former US Federal Reserve chief, admitted that he did not understand the complex derivative instruments that finally caused the meltdown. Therefore, there is a growing need to see the world through multiple lenses.

What would you advise India's leaders vis-à-vis China?

India's policy-makers should wake up to the rising concern about a growing trade deficit, especially with China. India's extremely large trade deficit with China can worsen in the coming years. This is not a good sign. It is a must to balance growth with liquidity, in fact, it is absolutely essential to build liquidity. Those who have the money call the shots. We need to set a target for achieving a positive trade surplus. That is really going to put us on the world economy's map. Leaders, both in business and in the government, need to market India with a more targeted approach.

Does the speed, or rather the lack of it, of decision-making by Indian leaders bother you?

The speed of change will continue to remain high. Leaders in business and government need to wake up to the fact that there is accelerated competition among nations and also to the fact that digitization and the use of algorithms are changing the composition of the world GDP. Digitization is destroying industries, but also creating opportunities for entrepreneurs. It will eventually boil down to how good is our decisiveness and it has to be high quality decisiveness. It is important to remember that businesses don't compete, leaders do. In China, there is decisiveness and there is speed in the execution of decisions. The differential in quality of decisiveness and the speed of execution will be a key determinant for India's growth. Temperament is very important. Remember, you can't clap with just one hand. We need to figure out how to do things together. That is why public-private partnership is important.

You have worked for more than 35 years behind the scenes with top executives at some of the world's most successful companies. What lesson would you give to small and medium entrepreneurs, who form the core of India's manufacturing sector?

We need to ask whether we are focusing enough on small and medium enterprises (SMEs), because these are the ones that are going to generate additional employment. It is important for us to nurture these enterprises.

GAURAV CHOUDHURY

'All firm heads are potential successors': ANAND MAHINDRA,

VICE-CHAIRMAN AND MD, M&M

He could well be the last chairman of the $15.4 billion group carrying the Mahindra surname. However, Anand Mahindra says it is more difficult to establish your credentials when you take on the mantle of the family business because people presume that you are here because of your last name. In an interview Mahindra says that one has to learn to swim against the tide. Excerpts:

How important is the Mahindra surname for the future of the Mahindra group?

Right now if you see, there is no relative of mine working here. My daughters are in different careers. One is a film maker and one is into designing. They are committed to their careers.

So, how does the succession planning system work in the Mahindra group?

The board has a nomination committee. Every manager in our system has to designate three people who can be his possible successor in a 'hit by bus scenario'. I have given some people's names to take over my responsibility. At the group level, if we look at the heads of each company, all of them are potential successors.

How easy or difficult was it for you to establish your credentials when you took charge of M&M?

It is more difficult to establish your credentials. People presume that you are here because of your last name. If somebody from the promoter family take up the job, it becomes doubly difficult. You come in with a handicap because people think that you have not earned the right to be here. Therefore at every stage you have to prove that you are there for legitimate reasons.

Did that mean a pressure to perform?

There was no pressure on me from outside. My undergraduate degree was in film making. Certainly if I would have gone into steel industry—my first job was in Mahindra Ugine—with a degree in film making, the credibility issue would have been much larger. I always joked that one of the reason why I went to Harvard Business School was to acquire credentials to be taken seriously. And that helped.

But is a B-school degree enough to run a business where often you need to rely on your gut feeling rather than excel spreadsheets?

There are incidents when an excel spreadsheet will tell you that this business will never turnaround. But the gut says this business will succeed.

For instance?

Scorpio rose out of an R&D project when we thought we 'can we make 13 seaters instead of a 10 seater'. Allan Durand, the head of our auto division, told me that one of our R&D executives had envisioned a product. When they showed it to me on screen, it almost looked 80% similar to the final Scorpio. Till then we had never done any hardtop other than Armada. The amount was also substantial—Rs 600 crore—the company had never invested that kind of money into any product; and we had never attempted a quantum leap in technology. Any left brain analysis would have advocated against it. At that time I had to take a decision.

How big a risk it was?

I was betting my job on the product, but not the company. If it failed I certainly would have lost my job. At that point it was pure gut instinct.

But you had taken riskier initiatives later, for example, your bid for JLR?

That is an example of how we look at risks. We were infact for a short time the preferred bidder for JLR. But we realised that even a 10% drop in sales would have involved huge amount of losses—far greater than the group could have afforded. That is why we never bet our company. Tatas went ahead and bid. I think next year there was huge decline in sales. Honestly, we would not have survived that. We are not as large a group as they are. In retrospect, what we did was right.

MANU P. TOMS AND TEJEESH N.S. BEHL

'A leader creates work culture for staff to excel': CHRISTOPHER BAILEY,

CHIEF CREATIVE OFFICER, BURBERRY

Burberry Kisses started with the idea of giving technology a heart and using it to enable people to express their love to each other across the globe by telling a story that makes the digital personal, says Christopher Bailey, chief creative officer of Burberry, who in his field of work doesn't restrict himself just to fashion designing and leads many such projects as Burberry Foundation, Burberry Acoustics and designing stores and offices for his brand. In an interview he said the ability to lead his team comes from creating a happy environment where everybody is functioning in a pleasant situation. Excerpts:

What do you think are the essential qualities of a leader, especially in the fashion/luxury world?

I feel that regardless of the field that you are in, the qualities that a leader should possess should be the same. For me, a leader must have compassion, ability to understand the team that he/she is heading and create a happy and pleasant working environment around him/her so as to make the team members perform and deliver nicely and comfortably.

What works for a leader? Elusiveness of designer Martin Margiela, popularity of Giorgio Armani or the way Tom Ford positions himself?

Well, they all are leaders in their own respective areas of work in the fashion and luxury industry. Various people have various means through which they reached their positions in their careers. For me, my ability to lead my team comes from a happy environment where everybody is functioning in a pleasant situation. As for personal traits of leaders, as you know, all leaders have different traits and in some way or the other it works for every one.

Who is that one leader who remains in your mind all along?

I must say that one man whom I hold in reverence for his leadership qualities is our chairman Sir John Peace. I have always tried to imbibe his compassion and understanding along with his ability to steer the brand to greater heights.

Unlike most other fashion designers, you always took several steps ahead when it comes to designing... You never stopped at clothes but lead yourself onto other areas?

When it comes to designing, I believe that it is the same for everything. Other than designing the collections, I have also designed Burberry's headquarters, the Horseferry House, in London, North America and Japan in addition to our flagship store at Regent Street London. In fact, soon Horseferry House II will also be operational here in London.

Joining hands with Google for Burberry Kisses was another attempt from your brand to lead the industry into innovations?

Well, I must say that Burberry Kisses project has been an interesting and rewarding experience. After having conceptualized it, it took me about three months to execute it through Google. Burberry Kisses, as you know, is the result of my attempt to bring in emotions in the world of technology…here one can send a kiss to his/her loved ones around the world and on the Burberry Kisses site map you could see the envelopes flying around from one city to the other around the world. And when I see the children sending kisses to their parents, it makes me happy.

What prompted you to go for such an innovation with Google?

Burberry Kisses is designed to entertain and engage global audiences through personalized and beautifully rendered content. Part of Google's 'Art, Copy & Code' initiative, it reflects a shared vision of humanizing technology through emotive digital experiences. Burberry Kisses began with the idea of giving technology a bit of heart and soul, and using it to unite the Burberry family across the world by telling a story that makes the digital space personal.

For the past few years, particularly the past couple of years, you have been trying to lead the men's tailoring side?

Yes, that's correct. We have been emphasizing on the men's tailoring side in the recent past and this is one area which I want to strengthen further. Here we offer hand-finished suits in over forty fabrics through new interpretation of such classic patterns as Prince of Wales checks, herringbones, houndstooth and pinstripes. We have introduced in-store tailoring services where a tailoring specialist will take the customer through the collection and after the selection, the suit will arrive in the store in forty-eight hours.

All suits are made in Italy. Made in Italy is bit of a surprise for an English brand like Burberry...does that mean you believe that Italians are leaders in men's tailoring? Savile Row in London is world-famous for men's tailoring?

Well, the suits are designed here at the Burberry headquarters. And then tailored in Italy. This is not to say that we don't have the ability to tailor our suits. English tailoring is well known and appreciated the world over. But, I believe that each part in the making of a suit must be handled by specialists regardless of their base.

You design both men's and women's collections...which is more exciting and challenging for you?

Like I said before, design per sé is exciting and challenging enough for me. While designing for both men swear and womens wear; for me the essential part is that of designing. And it's exciting for me to do both!

What was the best decision that you have taken in your career?

I would say that my decision to join this brand was the best decision I have taken. It has been quite challenging, enjoyable and at the same time rewarding for me personally...

And the worst?

Frankly, I can't seem to think of any.

VINOD NAIR

'A leader can mobilize a country to achieve dreams'
C.P. KRISHNAN NAIR,

CHAIRMAN EMERITUS AND FOUNDER CHAIRMAN, HOTEL LEELA VENTURE LIMITED

From a freedom fighter, then an officer serving in the Indian Army, to a textile exporter to a leading hotelier, the late Capt. C.P. Krishnan Nair has experienced from the ringside the country's economy for several decades. He spoke on a range of issues on leadership in an interview. Excerpts:

How do you define a leader?

I think a great leader has the courage to stand up for ideas or a dream and has the ability to mobilize a team, a country or a movement to achieve it. A leader inspires others to be the best they are capable of and see not only the vision but realize it also. Our culture has been thinking and writing about leadership for 3,000 years—from Lord Rama to King Ashoka to Mahatma Gandhi—and has given leaders different definitions.

What are the three most important traits of a leader?

I think the three most important traits of a leader are—determination, innovation, and audacity.

Can leadership be learnt? In other words, how can a manager become a leader?

Yes, leadership like all skills can be taught and learned. Over the course of my career, I have had the privilege to meet leaders like Mahatma Gandhi, Khan Abdul Gafar Khan also known as the Frontier Gandhi, and the Dalai Lama. I have met presidents and prime ministers from around the world including President (Barack) Obama and the late Baroness Margaret Thatcher, and virtually all business leaders of our time. Despite leading different countries, corporations, and movements, I found one quality that they all had in common is what I call 'leadership charisma'. This quality is self-learned and comes from a deep sense of meaning and fulfillment in one's work and by working effectively with others. On a macro level, an organization can help their managers become leaders by not only assessing where the managers are today but where they will be tomorrow.

What is the role of a professional leader in a promoter-driven company?

What I have learned through my own experiences as a textile innovator and a hotelier is that a successful leader is a powerful communicator. Too many strategies never get executed because they remain closely guarded secrets of the promoter's team. The leader's communication is what inspires a company to execute ideas and stand out and above from the rest.

As the leader of the Leela Group, how do you cultivate leaders?

Leaders are not born...they are made. I have individual relationships not just with my top team and managers but also with my gardeners and guards across our properties. And, I constantly communicate our core value—'Atithi Devo Bhava'—treat every guest like God, to all of them. At The Leela, we cultivate leadership by creating synergies between individual career pathways and the company's larger ethos, which prepares them for upward mobility within the organization and practice what we call the 'Leela Dharma'—which is a doctrine of duties to be followed by each employee.

Since September 2008, the world has fallen into a maelstrom of serial crises. What is the role of a leader in these times?

The mettle of a leader is often tested during a crisis. Global economic woes have triggered a wave of thinking about changes that need to be brought in organizational leadership, not just in banks and brokerages, but businesses in every industry. The role of a leader in these times is to become a powerful catalyst for change in the practice of leadership and corporate governance.

What has been the biggest leadership challenge you've faced?

Each of our properties was a challenge built against nearly insurmountable odds, and contrary to the conventional wisdom of the time. Most recently, I would say, it was building the first new hotel in the heart of the capital's diplomatic enclave.

Do you think the role of business leaders has come under cloud—globally and domestically—of late?

No, I don't think so. Indian business leaders have shaped the course of India and radically changed the business scenario internationally.

Leaders have to often carry the cross of other's wrongdoings and inefficiencies. What role can good leadership play to counterbalance this image?

When good people make bad decisions, it's because they are a part of a bad collective process. Good leadership now must provoke new thinking and new processes. The next generation of leaders should have the perspective, the mentality, the confidence, and the authority to call for a radical change.

What is your one line leadership mantra?

A lifelong inspiration for me has been the rallying call Pandit Jawarharlal Nehru made to the nation: 'Success comes to those who dare and act.'

Who are the leaders that have inspired you?

Subhash Chandra Bose, VP Menon, the 14th Dalai Lama.

Who is a leader in your industry that your respect?

I have tremendous respect for all the leaders in my industry.

What is the biggest leadership lesson that you have learnt?

In every crisis lies an opportunity.

What is the best leadership decision you have taken?

The best decision I made was opening a Palace hotel in the heart of New Delhi. I believe that to be a hospitality player to reckon with, a prominent presence in our capital is very important.

What is the worst leadership decision you have taken?

Weak performances test my patience. Probably the worst leadership decision I have taken was tolerating a weak performance longer than I should have.

'Leaders open avenues':
DEEPAK KAPOOR,
CHAIRMAN, PRICEWATERHOUSECOOPERS

Deepak Kapoor, chairman, PricewaterhouseCoopers (PwC) India, an auditing and management consulting major, spoke on a range of issues in an interview. He spoke at length on his trying experience of handling the crisis following the stunning confessions of the erstwhile Satyam Computer Services' chairman that the company's books were doctored for several years.

How do you define a leader?

I believe leadership is all about people. A leader is one who makes sure people not only see the vision, but live and breathe it. They inspire others to be the best that they are capable of. A leader is also one who represents the spirit of a brand.

What are the three most important traits of a leader?

A leader needs to be a motivator, one who inspires trust and spurs others to perform. Their foresight charts a course for the future and navigates the organization through it successfully. They should be good at listening, should be able to empathize and effectively empower their people.

As the leader of PwC in India, how do you cultivate leaders?

It is very important for an organization to nurture tomorrow's leaders. Of the many leadership programmes that we currently have at PwC, one that stands out is the Young Partners Forum. This platform gives select young partners, on a rotation basis, the opportunity to deliberate and recommend on live issues facing the firm. These recommendations are then considered by the leadership team whose decisions are communicated back to the young partners, giving them insights into why the leadership team took the decisions it did, taking them a step or two higher in their transition towards 'hard' leadership skills. Also, at PwC, diversity is at the core of our business philosophy. We value the unique qualities of leadership that come from our women colleagues, and actively promote them. We have worked hard at plugging the leaking talent pipeline, and it gives me pride to tell you that currently 30% of our employees are women. We also have 19 women leaders as partners/executive directors and directors, and 19% of our leadership team consists of women too.

Can leadership be learnt? Like, how can a manager become a leader?

Absolutely! A good manager can evolve into a good leader by working effectively with teams and most importantly by developing skills which can help them unlock other people's potential.

Since September 2008, the world has fallen into a maelstrom of serial crises. What is the role of a leader in these times?

It is in tough times that the mettle of a leader is tested. Instead of becoming defensive, good leaders take steps to improve their businesses' resilience against further disruptions and to grow in markets they believe are most important for their future. They lead the process of crafting new approaches to risk management and new strategies in response. Also, they make sure that there is right talent at the right place.

What has been the biggest leadership challenge you've faced?

The Satyam episode. The challenge was to convince our clients, staff and the community that the audit team was misled by the Satyam management, and no one from our staff was involved in the fraud perpetrated by the erstwhile Satyam's promoters/senior management. Though it took time and effort to win back the trust of our stakeholders, I am happy to say that we overcame this challenge and soon rebuilt the reputation as providers of high quality in our chosen line of service.

Do you think the role of business leaders have come under a cloud—globally and domestically—of late?

As long as a leader conducts business ethically, within the framework of applicable professional standards, laws, and regulations, there is no reason for this to happen. Of course, as the scale of operations increase, more issues will crop up, but these are opportunities for us to keep plugging the gaps.

Leaders have to often carry the cross of other's wrong doings and inefficiencies, the global banking sector today, for instance. What role can good leadership play to counterbalance this image?

As mentioned earlier, one of the roles of a leader is prudent risk management. Disruptions in the environment could be because of other's actions, but good leaders will have their own business environment as insulated as possible.

What is your one-line leadership mantra?

It is the responsibility of leadership to provide opportunity, and the responsibility of individuals to contribute.

Who are the leaders that have inspired you?

Martin Luther King Jr., minister and leader of the American Civil Rights Movement, and Mahatma Gandhi.

Who is a leader in your industry that you respect?

I will take the liberty of extending this beyond my industry, JRD Tata is someone who has been an inspirational business leader for me.

What is the biggest leadership lesson that you have learnt?

Appearance and content are two different things. Don't be quick to pass judgment.

What is the best leadership decision you have taken?

Succession planning and initiatives to focus on the development of our high performers, creation of the Young Partners Forum being one of these.

What is the worst leadership decision you have taken?

I could have taken a few decisions like 'not tolerating less than desired performance' faster, but as they say, it's never too late!

GAURAV CHOUDHURY

'Effective leaders are great listeners': BARRY SALZBERG,

CEO, DELOITTE TOUCHE TOHMATSU

B arry Salzberg is the global CEO of consulting major Deloitte Touche Tohmatsu Limited, Salzberg leads and manages the $31 billion company that consists of 47 member firms operating in 150 countries and employs around 2,00,000 people worldwide. Excerpts from an interview:

How do you define leadership?

The concept of leadership has changed over the years. It used to be about the person in charge of an organization, a business or an operation. It is now more about the team. It consists of picking the right team that maximizes the performance of a diverse group of individuals and being able to lead the team. Leadership is all about playing together to drive organizational goals.

What are three key attributes of a leader?

Effective leaders are great listeners. They know how to ask the right questions, gather inputs and distil the best information from many sources. Leaders have loads of experience and so they should have the ability to share experiences and mentor others. I think there should be something unique about a leader—subject expertise or personality trait—that makes him unusually appealing. I call it 'branding'. Good leaders tend to brand themselves.

As the leader of a global organization, how do you cultivate leaders?

It is about providing an environment of learning. So, it is important to create the mindset that learning matters, and to create an environment that encourages individuals with high potential and high performance to take advantage of that mindset. I spent time with my direct reportees all the time. When I am in another country, I spent time with the individual CEO and other leaders of that country. There isn't anything that I am doing to teach. There isn't anything that I am doing to provide leadership development right there. It is the interaction to share best practices and to engage in a dialogue that matter in strategy and execution. To develop and cultivate leaders, a CEO has to spend time with individuals one-on-one and in groups.

Can leadership be learnt? How can a manager become a leader?

I think it can be both. I think there are natural born leaders. I don't know whether it is DNA, upbringing, value system or environment that makes natural leaders. On the other hand, I think many people are born with attributes that can be further developed. There are attributes of leadership that can be groomed. There are elements of leadership that can be enhanced. Therefore leadership development is important. If everybody is born with leadership skills you don't need to do anything. But that is not the case.

What has been the biggest leadership challenge you've faced?

There are many. The biggest one I faced as a leader was during the economic crisis of 2007–2008—leading an organization through an economic crisis as well as what was really a crisis in capital markets. It was a challenge to retain confidence and optimism that this isn't the end and to create the roadmap for the future and manage our way through the internally difficult operations because if we don't produce, our partners won't take anything home. At that time I was heading the US operations and we were significantly off our revenue target. And, my challenge was how best we can produce results, how best we can maintain our quality and commitment.

How did you deal with the challenge?

First, I properly planned. We did a lot of work previously. We had some foresight US might go through an economic difficulty. Preparation was the key. Secondly, what helped was what I call tunnel vision—you are not distracted by anything and work relentlessly to drive a solution. Thirdly, communication—the best thing to do is openly share challenges. We have done well. Deloitte today is performing better today compared to economic crisis five years ago. We have made some very difficult decisions along the way to produce some very good results.

Since September 2008, the world has fallen into a maelstrom of serial crises. What is the role of a leader in these times?

It is to provide a sense of optimism, 'can do' and progress. To create that comfort in people that they need. Typically, when going through a crisis, people are nervous. They are concerned about their jobs and about the ability of the organization to help them. Leader needs to steer the ship and provide calm and optimism.

Do you think the role of business leaders has come under cloud of late?

Definitely, there is a need of business leaders to stand out and create a higher level of trust and credibility. I think in this uncertain environment it is extremely important to create a further commitment to trust among all stakeholders, whether regulators, shareholders or public at large. The fundamental responsibility of a leader is to restore that trust.

What's your one line leadership mantra?

I've coined a phrase: 'five Ps'. Proper planning prevents poor performance.

Who are the leaders that've inspired you?

Jack Welch is a big inspiration. I created Deloitte University for leadership and training, under his influence. Collin Powell, an African American political leader, has inspired me with books and speeches on leadership.

What is your best leadership decision?

To build Deloitte University, The Leadership Center which opened in October 2011 in Westlake, Texas. We were going through a difficult phase economically and so not many were convinced about it. It required an investment of $300 million to build a 700,000+ square foot campus that provides enriching experiences for our people and to ensure Deloitte remains a place where leaders thrive and ideas prosper. Deloitte is committed to growing leadership skills at every level of the organization and to this day I have partners writing back to me saying we actually do what we promised to deliver through this center. It was an investment in people, leadership and building the right culture for Deloitte.

…And the worst?

To have appointed a few wrong people in leadership positions and not acting on it quickly was a wrong decision.

MANU P TOMS

'A leader should be lively and active': FRANCK DARDENNE,

COUNTRY HEAD, LVMH WATCH & JEWELLERY INDIA PVT LTD

Franck Dardenne, country head, LVMH Watch & Jewellery India Pvt Ltd, the Indian arm of French luxury goods conglomerate, has got his timing right in India. Dardenne is the man behind selling premium watches—TAG Heuer, Dior and Zenith—ranging from Rs 1 lakh to Rs 1.7 crore in India. He started his career, as a marketing analyst and has been with the LVMH Group since 2002. Dardenne talks about selling premium watches to price-sensitive Indians. Excerpts from an interview:

What is leadership for you?

It's about having a vision and inspiring a team to reach that vision. Being clear of what you want, makes one a leader.

Being a French, how a leader adapts to the cultural barriers?

The first difficulty I faced in India was to make my English understood despite the French accent. But, now this difficulty is over. I have understood that a leader is best when he/she is respectful and authentic and remains who he/ she actually is. He/ she should be able to impart clear and frank indications, stop being artificial, and open the set of appreciation and criticism in front of colleagues and seniors.

What is the best leadership decision that you have taken so far?

Providing strong support to my partners, over the past year, when they faced difficult situations has been my best decision. This also proved that despite a direct way of conducting business—with a will to implement clear guidelines to pay tribute to our brands—the clients found us on their side. It didn't just benefit our brands, but also helped the overall watch industry.

And, your worst decision as a leader?

I committed the mistake of wanting to do many things at a time. I took time to understand that one shouldn't do things, just to do them. I always disliked things done in an imperfect manner. Now, I have learnt to be patient. On the other hand, in a country like India, it is important to use patience as the market is new, and I should wait till the situation matures.

Is there a difference in leadership style when you manage business in India (a developing nation where luxury is still penetrating) and when you manage business in Europe?

Since leadership implies convincing colleagues and partners, one must adapt to the communication style of the respective country. Business style in India is warmer than in some other countries. Partners are hardworking and promising. However, relationships are critical. Nevertheless, I don't think that special features of one country really impacts what is at the heart of the leadership.

Does organization plays a crucial role in drafting your leadership style?

Indeed. Being clear on what is needed by the organization is most beneficial, even if it implies to close some points of sales. Your set of values and perspectives should be moulded in accordance to the need of organization.

Being a leader of a famous luxury watch house, how do you keep yourself updated about the fashion trends around the globe?

I visit watch shops half of my working time and talk to the staff and the retailers. It is the most efficient way to keep oneself updated.

Has any Indian leader, sportsperson or corporate leader, you have taken notice of, inspired you in some sense?

I still don't know many Indians, but I keep meeting Shah Rukh Khan (Bollywood actor). He is an incredibly charismatic person and is capable of infusing energy across the environment. Like him, a leader should be known for his charisma and energy. He should not be dull and dark; he must be very lively and active.

Euro zone has been tumultuous. How do you handle bad economic scenario while managing the press enquiries, organization's expectations and your inner goals?

A leader must be a good planner and good executor. Role of leadership is proved during the time of crises. Many good leaders go for a toss, and bad leaders arrive, just because of the capacity to deliver while everyone else is broken. Like for say, in India, the watch market has been impacted, however, it still grew by 9% in 2012. A leader should have clarity about the brand positioning, innovation and good distribution that makes a brand successful.

Who is your greatest inspiration?

My inspiration is related to 11 years of working in TAG Heuer. The result-oriented drive of the TAG Heuer president, Jean-Christophe Babin, has been a fantastic source of inspiration. At other times, Jack Heuer, great grandson of Edouard Heuer, founder of TAG Heuer, has also been a great source of inspiration.

Where does India stand for you in the list of countries you look to expand business in?

We invest a lot in India because we believe from the present 24th position in the luxury watch market, it will soon be in the top 10. It's already better in the ranking of our brands. Of course, we don't know when there will be a boom for luxury goods but, one day, it will come and we will then receive the dividend of our investments.

How do you plan to penetrate further in India?

It depends on the strategy and the maturity of the brands. In the case of Dior, which is available at Rs 3 lakh and above, penetration implies narrowing the network. In the case of Zenith, present at 6 points of sales and launched in September 2010, the main focus is the top three metros. Many retailers want this brand, which is good, but before expanding the distribution, we want to become successful with a limited number of doors. Regarding TAG Heuer, we are present in 27 cities, and we may still expand to a few more, but not too much. Even if TAG Heuer is now known all over the territory and is a leading watch brand in India, productivity per door will be our main focus, together with expansion through opening some boutiques. TAG Heuer plans to add seven new boutiques in 2013 taking the total number to 13.

HIMANI CHANDNA GURTOO

'A leader carves the future':
PIYUSH MATHUR,

PRESIDENT, INDIA, THE NIELSEN COMPANY

Piyush Mathur, president, India, The Nielsen Company, a global leader in market research, says if you are simple in everything you do, most people understand you and you give them a chance of making a difference. Mathur spoke on a range of leadership issues in an interview. Excerpts:

How do you define a leader?

Being able to unlock the potential of talent, which even the talent can't imagine.

What are the three most important traits of a leader?

Being open, simple and integrated. I believe if you are open to feedback, you build trust. If you are simple in everything you do (it's the hardest thing to do), most people understand you and you give them a chance of making a difference. If you are integrated internally within the organization and externally with various stakeholders, you have a network that increases your odds of success.

As a leader of your group, how do you cultivate leaders?

We build our leaders through building our culture. Although it's difficult to assess how the culture is getting built, we look at whether our colleagues know what to do without being told what to do. We build our culture around open, simple and integrated leadership traits and assess whether we are getting better on them with every passing year. Culture can truly be a key differentiator in your industry.

Can leadership be learnt? In other words, how can a manager become a leader?

Yes, it can be learnt end to end. I will remain a student of leadership for the rest of my life. I think a manager becomes a leader when he makes his team members better than him, especially on leadership.

What is the role of a professional leader in a promoter-driven company?

I believe his role is to build a professional organization. Sometimes promoter-driven companies may not follow the principles of meritocracy, may not imbibe simple, open, integrated traits. He needs to build a culture that attracts professional talent to the organization and be able to take on any best-in-class multinational organization.

Since September 2008, the world has fallen into a maelstrom of serial crises. What is the role of a leader in these times?

A crisis makes a good leader great. I believe a crisis provides the opportunity to take unprecedented strides in leadership but often, leaders only see it as a challenge and look at it as an opportunity,

So, when you are in the hot seat, you remain cool and continue to build your organization step by step.

What has been the biggest leadership challenge you have faced?

As I took my India assignment three years ago, one of my biggest challenges was to build a culture of meritocracy. I have seen this lacking in many organizations in India, where not enough differentiation is done between high and low performers. I truly believe if you retain your top talent, it will be very difficult for you to fail. At Nielsen, meritocracy is fast becoming part of our DNA and twice a year, we look at both performance and leadership potential for all of our 3,000+ associates in India. I can see the needle moving, but obviously it's a journey, not a destination.

Do you think the role of business leaders has come under cloud—globally and domestically—of late?

No. I just believe that the environment has helped in distinguishing great leaders from not-so-great leaders. Like I said, if leaders look at the recent global crisis as an opportunity to stand out from the pack, then they are on their way to converting challenges into growth for their companies and being on cloud nine rather than being under the cloud!

Leaders have to often carry the cross of other's wrongdoings and inefficiencies, the global banking sector today, for instance. What role can good leadership play to counterbalance this image?

A leader only carves the future rather than crib about the past. He needs to look through the front glass, accept the present position and start building his GPS to get to the position that is the vision for the industry and for the company.

What is your one line leadership mantra?

'It takes teamwork to make our dream work.'

What is the biggest leadership lesson that you have learnt?

Focus on your strengths, blunt your weaknesses. If you build your career on your strengths, you are likely to enjoy your work, be more successful and be happier in your life.

GAURAV CHOUDHURY

'A leader must develop talent': YASMINE HILTON,
CHAIRMAN, SHELL INDIA

Yasmine Hilton is the first woman chairman to be heading one of India's biggest multinational energy companies—Shell India. After serving 30 years in the company in various roles, she says this will be her last job. She spoke on the responsibilities and challenges faced by a leader. Excerpts from an interview:

How do you define a leader?

I think a good leader is someone who can inspire all the employees of an organization to deliver exceptional results—now and in the future—sustainability is the key.

What are the three most important traits of a leader?

First, the ability to develop a shared vision, carrying everyone in the enterprise; second, being able to deliver results as promised, or beyond; and third, the ability to inspire and develop talent—recognizing in people potential that they do not realize they have. If a leader can do this, it is tremendously motivational. In the end it's about inclusive teamwork—a good leader knows that to be successful he or she needs to have the whole organization pulling together effectively.

As a leader of your group, how do you cultivate leaders?

By devoting a lot of time to working with people, observing and helping them—coaching, encouraging and giving honest feedback. Everyone needs help and support to grow and develop, and I enjoy this aspect of my job very much. Seeing people improve their skills and confidence gives me great satisfaction. It makes my job easier in the long run and is good for the enterprise. Time spent mentoring staff is rarely wasted.

Can leadership be learnt? In other words, how can a manager become a leader?

Yes, I believe so. People aren't born to lead—a manager can become a leader provided that he or she has the drive, application and willingness to learn and adapt. It is important to be able to see the big picture over a longer time horizon to build a sustainable organization. A little humility and empathy for people and above all an ability to be decisive, having listened to and considered other views, go a long way.

What is the role of a professional leader in a promoter-driven company?

It is not a role I am familiar with. But any large successful organization has to attract and retain talent and that cannot be done effectively without professionalism and good stakeholder management. It's a universal truth.

Since September 2008, the world has fallen into a maelstrom of serial crises. What is the role of a leader in these times?

It is a volatile world and there have been serial crises before 2008 as well; the energy business has had many shocks over the years. Keeping the big picture and a long-term vision in mind are important. Leaders need to be able to respond calmly in a crisis, steady the ship and act decisively. Being prepared, using scenarios and crisis management techniques are important.

What has been the biggest leadership challenge you've faced?

Well, there have been many—that's what I love about working in Shell. You get the chance to move across functions, businesses and countries. My previous role was chief information officer (CIO) of Shell's global retail business, stretching over five continents. We had a poor track record at delivering major multi-million dollar global projects on time and on budget. My team turned this around, and we were benchmarked at top quartile after three years. Reaching this milestone proved a tough challenge—and it was a proud moment for the organization. It is now in their DNA.

Do you think the role of business leaders has come under cloud -globally and domestically—of late?

Every era has its challenges and every company has problems from time to time, no matter how well-run they are. In Shell, we have a strong code of conduct and everyone must comply with 'Shell Business Principles', with their emphasis on health, safety, security and the environment (HSSE), ethics and compliance. For me, this makes life simpler.

Leaders have to often carry the cross of others' wrongdoings and inefficiencies—the global banking sector today, for instance. What role can a good leader play to counterbalance this image?

I think good leadership means running your own business well in the interests of all your stakeholders, communicating clearly what you are doing, while playing the role of a good citizen within the community. Reputation is built over decades and can be destroyed in a moment. It's the responsibility of every business leader to be aware of this and act accordingly.

What is your one-line leadership mantra?

Always deliver on your promises.

Who are the leaders who have inspired you?

There have been many in my own company, who are not household names. I have learnt more personally from people that I worked with than iconic industry leaders, much as I may admire them. Shell is a company that offers many opportunities, takes some risks with appointments and supports people while they develop and are growing in the job. I was the first professional woman to work part-time while my kids were young and even reached the position of CIO in Shell UK on this basis. I am inspired to do the same for others so that they too can fulfil their potential.

Who is a leader in your industry whom you respect?

With my original information technology background, I would say Bill Gates and Azim Premji—both for their creativity and their philanthropy.

What is the biggest leadership lesson that you have learnt?

Treat people with respect and support them, but do not tolerate under performance.

What is the best leadership decision you have taken?

All the tough ones. You never regret taking tough decisions and those are usually the best ones, when you look back.

What is the worst leadership decision you have taken?

The ones I did not take quickly enough, allowing situations to run on for too long. Lesson learned.

Do you see India as a challenging market vis-a-vis other markets?

I believe India has huge potential, with exciting, innovative young talent emerging all over the country. It's challenging, yes, and India may not be the easiest country to do business in. However, it is slowly, inexorably moving to a level playing field where open access, deregulation and a consistent and transparent framework will become the order of the day. I believe Shell's technical and commercial best practices can make a real contribution to meeting India's energy challenges. India has some way to go to become a place where foreign investors feel welcome. Business growth and people growth go hand-in-hand. That's why I believe India has a bright future—and why I was delighted to take on this job.

ANUPAMA AIRY

'A leader should be a people-centric person': NIKHIL NANDA,

JOINT MANAGING DIRECTOR, ESCORTS LTD

Nikhil Nanda, joint managing director, Escorts Ltd, has the overall responsibility for managing the group's agriculture, construction and engineering businesses. Nanda, an alumnus of Wharton Business School, Philadelphia, spoke on a range of issues on leadership. Excerpts from an interview:

How do you define a leader?

For me a leader has to have passion, an attitude and a correct state of mind. He should be able to crystallize the vision that needs to be achieved by the group of followers. A leader must give his people a sense of purpose, an objective to achieve, and be able to rally people towards this cause. He should be able to push the envelope and refuse to accept anything remotely close to mediocrity. A leader has to depict courage in action. A leader is someone who inspires a team of followers by earning their trust and respect by setting a good example and being competent at what he does. A leader makes tough decisions and prepares the team for the stress that will follow. He motivates them in times of change and manages the change in order to help the team achieve the collective goal.

What are the three most important traits of a leader?

I would say interpersonal skills, passion and spontaneity. To be a successful leader, you have to have traits of being a people-centric person. Passion is the fire in you to pursue your goals and make it clear to everyone what is important and what is not. Thirdly, he has to be spontaneous in a way. That is, he should have the capacity to weigh conflicting options, to be able to make hard choices when both options are good or bad. It is about mental agility.

As a leader of the Escorts Group, how do you cultivate leaders?

At Escorts, we seek out to people with potential, who are creating positive changes, even in small ways. Leadership programs are held at selected intervals for senior and mid-management levels that encourage co-ownership, bring about cross-pollination and thought leadership.

Can leadership be learnt? In other words, how can a manager become a leader?

Absolutely, yes. Leadership can be both, learnt and cultivated. Some people are natural leaders but that doesn't mean others cannot be. Strong people skills, having a clear vision of your goals and genuinely working towards it, and also inspiring others to achieve the same are just a few traits that can help one step up the ladder.

What is the role of a professional leader in a promoter-driven company?

The role of a leader is to motivate people around him, engage with employees in a way that resembles an ordinary person-to-person conversation, more than a series of commands from top officials. It's the professional leader that gives shape to the entrepreneurial drive of the promoters and gives an institutionalized framework for achieving the goals set. This is critical to building an institution.

Since September 2008, the world has fallen into a maelstrom of serial crises. What is the role of a leader in these times?

Every crisis is an opportunity in itself. The prime role during a crisis would be not to let negativity creep in the organization. Motivate the employees to believe in themselves and the organization. The fundamental principles of an organization must always remain strong, the core values must never be compromised and one must invest in product development that enhances the value to the customers.

What has been the biggest leadership challenge you've faced?

Taking care of 15,000 employees is not an easy job. If you are not able to motivate them, you are a failure from day one. Shouldering this responsibility is my passion. Some of the biggest challenges are to bring about a cultural shift, break old habits and old mindsets and make space for the team members to bring in an innovative culture that allows for mistakes. Fulfilling all this in a collaborative environment is a challenge in itself.

What is your one-line leadership mantra?

To create an environment and a culture that brings out the best in individuals. To achieve that, my focus is to create values within the organization.

Who are the leaders that have inspired you?

The beacon for me has been my grandfather, H.P. Nanda. In many ways he was 'tomorrow's man'. He always carried a visionary approach to his decision making and instinctively knew that if not today, the benefits would flow tomorrow. People placed their trust in him, even as he exhorted them to excel, always knowing that he was there for them. He and JRD Tata, another person who has been a big inspiration for me, were contemporaries. They were both fearless leaders who were focussed on not just creating a company but with that bringing a change in their society.

What is the biggest leadership lesson that you have learnt?

That leadership is not about 'you'. It's about building your people and your company. We as leaders are mere custodians to ensure the continuity and purpose of the enterprise.

What is the best leadership decision you have taken?

My best decision would be that to surround myself with the most competent team and ensure to harvest their talents and in the process meet the aspirations of building a great enterprise for the future.

What is the worst leadership decision you have taken?

Mistakes are inevitable since they help you shape up as a mature and balanced leader. So we make mistakes in our day-to-day lives. I learn from my mistakes, though I can't recall a mistake that's hounding me even now. I have a tendency to listen more than talk. So, before I take a decision, I ensure that I'm surrounded by people whom I respect in terms of their talent and experience. So decision-making, to that extent, becomes easier. That consensus, perhaps, helps in reducing mistakes.

GAURAV CHOUDHURY

'A leader must enter office to earn respect': AJAY BIJLI,

CHAIRMAN AND MD, PVR LTD

Ajay Bijli, chairman and managing director, PVR Ltd, commenced his entrepreneur career by pioneering the multiplex revolution in India. A Harvard Business School alumnus and a Hindu College graduate, Bijli harboured his ambitions to provide the best of movie entertainment to Indian audience, who had long been starved of quality cinema viewing experience. He spoke about various leadership issues. Excerpts from an interview:

How do you define a leader?

A true leader possesses diverse qualities. He needs to be able to articulate a clear vision and set realistic organizational goals. A motivator, great orator and listener, he practices what he preaches. He should be humble but not self-effacing, disciplined in his approach and display high integrity.

What are the most important traits of a leader?

He must be able to define a clear vision that's challenging, must command respect by having the integrity and skills to manage all stakeholders effectively.

As a leader of your group, how do you cultivate leaders?

By giving them responsibility, empowerment and space to operate.

Can leadership be learnt? In other words, how can a manager become a leader?

Even if people say that they are born leaders, they still need to constantly hone their skills to lead. You constantly need to learn and enhance your leadership skills. Managers can be leaders with proper training but they need to display some important traits of leadership qualities early on.

What is the role of a leader in times of economic crisis?

It is important for him to ensure that his team is aware of and fully geared up to face any adversity. He should be armed with a clear-cut action plan to take care of external and internal issues to ensure the ship stays afloat. And this is where equanimity is important—leaders need to show composure.

What has been the biggest leadership challenge you've faced?

It has been a 23-year-old journey so far. The most epochal one for me has been my father's unexpected demise. It was a very unfortunate way to get to learn how to handle things at the helm of affairs.

Do you think the role of business leaders has come under cloud —globally and domestically—of late?

I don't think so. There are several inspirational leaders who have created iconic companies. As long as leaders run their businesses with integrity and sincerity with a view to creating businesses that touch people's lives and don't compromise on business ethics while doing so, there are no dark shadows to be cast.

What is your one-line leadership mantra?

Enter the office every day to earn respect and reputation—that's how wealth will be created.

Who is a leader in your industry that your respect?

Walt Disney.

What is the biggest leadership lesson that you have learnt?

Be humble, a lot was accomplished before you were born.

What has been your best leadership decision till now?

If I were to choose one in recent times, the Cinemax acquisition was an important one for PVR. I am glad we were able to succeed that created a clear distinction in the exhibition industry in terms of quality and quantity.

And, the worst decision?

Again, I never evaluate decisions in those terms. Perhaps trying to diversify into multiple verticals at a very early stage of our journey at the cost of our core business may not have been a good idea.

GAURAV CHOUDHURY

'Integrity defines foundation of leadership': SANJAY RISHI,

PRESIDENT, AMERICAN EXPRESS SOUTH ASIA

Belief in a purpose, the courage and conviction to pursue it relentlessly, the ability to motivate individuals and teams, the creativity and risk orientation to try new things and a growth mindset that constantly reminds you that the learning process never stops are the hallmark of a leader, says Sanjay Rishi, president, American Express South Asia. In an interview, he said that leading is a way of being and there is no need to have direct reports to demonstrate leadership, instead you earn your space through competence, caring and judgement. Excerpts:

How do you define a leader?

In the words of Robert F Kennedy, 'progress is a nice word, but change is a motivator'. And, when Mahatma Gandhi said, 'We must be the change we want to see in the world,' I think he was really talking about the essence of leadership. Belief in a purpose, the courage and conviction to pursue it relentlessly, the ability to motivate individuals and teams, the creativity and risk orientation to try new things, a growth mindset that constantly reminds you that the learning process never stops and above all, the wisdom to anchor yourself in humility, knowing that it's not about you, it's about the cause you serve and it's about shining a light on your people who help make it happen. That's what leadership is about.

What are the three most important traits of a leader?

Our CEO, Kenneth Chennault, reminds us that 'reputations are truly made or lost in a crisis' and that points to the first trait of a good leader. The second trait is about the idea that intelligence and potential are not static and one's skills can be cultivated through effort, application and experience, no matter what your age, education or position is. The third trait is integrity. Integrity defines the foundation of leadership, as consistency in values and action is critical to build trusting relationships.

As a leader of your group, how do you cultivate leaders?

At American Express everyone is considered to be a leader. Leading is a way of being and you don't need to have direct reports to demonstrate leadership, instead you earn your space through competence, caring and judgement.

Can leadership be learnt? In other words, how can a manager become a leader?

Absolutely. What is imperative is that to earn the privilege to lead requires hard work, practice, the ability to learn and constant feedback. Some of the 'watch outs' are to expect the title of 'leader' as an entitlement because of tenure or seniority.

Since September 2008, the world has fallen into a maelstrom of serial crises. What is the role of a leader in these times?

True leadership is tested during a time of crisis or change. This is the time when leaders are more closely scrutinized.

Do you think the role of business leaders has come under a cloud both globally and domestically of late?

The role of modern-day leaders is complicated around the world. There are challenges in the form of managing requirements of government, expectations of stakeholders and most importantly, maintaining the curve ahead of the competition. The role of good business leaders is more important than ever before and I wouldn't say it's come under a cloud.

How important is leadership, especially in the non-profit sector?

Today, philanthropy is about real outcomes. To get funding, NGOs are expected to talk about innovations, measure of success and impact just like any private company would. We all know that the stakes are very high for business but I believe that stakes are higher for social sectors because they deal with people's lives, and therefore, they can't let performance slide. At American Express, through the Leadership Academy our endeavor is to create an effective programme to help understand the needs of the sector and bridge gaps with a vision to develop a broader pool of world-class leaders committed to development. We feel that management and leadership skills existing in the corporate sector can be adopted by non-profit sector leaders to support and strengthen their contribution to society.

What has been the biggest leadership challenge you've faced?

Initially, I struggled with introducing change in a situation where there was no immediate burning platform calling for it. Yet, the change was necessary to protect and strengthen our franchise over the next five to seven years. I learnt through the process the importance of setting the context and creating a sense of purpose.

GAURAV CHOUDHURY

'A leader must have selfless agenda': SURINDER KAPUR,

FOUNDER CHAIRMAN, SONA GROUP

The late Surinder Kapur, founder chairman of Sona Group, which manufactures components for the automotive industry, had shared his leadership mantra in an interview. Excerpts:

How do you define a leader?

A leader is one who motivates his people by sharing his vision enthusiastically and in a believable way, so employees trust his leadership.

What are the three most important traits of a leader?

A leader should be a greater communicator and be able to: share vision and goals with the people; build and give hope to people, which also translates into trust; and align people together to achieve the collective vision.

As a leader of your group, how do you cultivate leaders?

We have a special programme called 'Drivers of Tomorrow' (DOT), which is being led by my son Sunjay Kapur. This is a fast track programme for potential leaders, which is conducted year round with both in-house and external faculty deployed to build and speak on the traits of leadership and cultivate leadership traits in the inductees. The idea is to transform a manager into a leader.

Can leadership be learnt? In other words, how can a manager become a leader?

Yes, I do believe that leadership can be learned. However, there are also people who are born leaders. But, it is not necessary that one cannot be a leader if he or she was not born with the leadership traits. Similarly, in the case of entrepreneurs, not all entrepreneurs end up as good leaders. Enough evidence exists today to suggest this fact. Entrepreneurs either sell off their businesses or bring in CEOs to run their businesses.

What has been the biggest leadership challenge you've faced?

During 2008 we bought a large company in Germany and turning that company around after the financial crisis was a real challenge. In a foreign country, with a foreign language, turning it around during the crisis was a tough challenge. I personally took the challenge, fired the existing management and visited Germany every month in the last three years, and the results were most satisfying. To overcome the language barrier, I used an interpreter. I communicated with my employees regularly, introduced discussion forums and formed a monthly monitoring meeting with my union leaders. I committed to not to let go of my 1,300 employees, was transparent about the financial health of the company, their poor performance on productivity, and slashed overheads dramatically.

Do you think the role of business leaders has come under cloud—globally and domestically—of late?

One of the main reasons for global financial crises, in my personal opinion, was excessive greed. This greed was mostly for personal gains, rather than for the organization's good. Business should not have only short-term gains but should rather work for creating shareholder value in the long-term. In my personal view, around 2005 to 2007, various global banks, corporate and governments allowed the decision-making to be biased by greed. The balanced leadership and clear objective were missing, which led to crisis.

Leaders have to often carry the cross of other's wrongdoings and inefficiencies, the global banking sector today, for instance. What role can good leadership play to counterbalance this image?

Leadership must have a selfless agenda. One cannot be a successful leader if he or she only thinks of personal gain. Leaders of today have to walk that extra mile to first clear the negatives associated and then come forth with a transparent approach. Having said that, one must accept that there have been flaws and issues, but a good leader will also communicate the possible remedies to tackle the impending issues. This will not only instil confidence in the followers but also help to garner strength and support from the team.

What is your one line leadership mantra?

Peddle 'hope' and create 'trust'.

Who are the leaders that have inspired you?

There are two leaders whom I have looked up to as my gurus and who have inspired me. They are my father-in-law the late Raunaq Singh, one of the greatest entrepreneurs I have known; and Keshub Mahindra (former chairman of the Mahindra Group), who is one of the best corporate leaders. Both of them were selfless in their way and 'karmacharis' in my personal view.

What is the biggest leadership lesson that you have learnt?

People will only follow and respect you as a leader if you can win their trust. This alone can be achieved by being transparent and having a vision that can motivate people.

What is the best leadership decision you have taken?

The best decision we took was of acquiring the forging businesses in Europe and the USA. At that time Sona Okegawa was a Rs 200 crore company, which went onto making acquisitions of Rs 2,500 crore.

What is the worst leadership decision you have taken?

I trusted the management of the European company, which we had acquired without conducting due diligence. As a result, the lesson learnt was that sometimes a leader must also micro manage.

'A leader should leave legacies': ANIL SARDANA,

MANAGING DIRECTOR, TATA POWER

A nil Sardana, managing director of Tata Power, believes changing Delhi's corruption-ridden system was a big leadership challenge. He spoke on a range of issues on leadership. Excerpts from an interview:

How do you define a leader?

A leader is the one who has passion to leave legacies, for which posterity would remember his contribution. A leader must thus build teams, which share his conviction and remain motivated to deliver their best. A leader has to be a friend, a philosopher and a guide in true sense of every word. Emotional intelligence is a key attribute required for a leader as empathy, social skills and self-awareness are key skill sets required to distinguish an outstanding performer from others.

What are the three most important traits of a leader?

I would say that clearly defining the goals and objectives and aligning each of the teammate for a shared vision; thereafter pursuing and engaging teams to deliver the best; thirdly, putting in place a cycle of continuous learning and improvement are the traits that a good leader must possess and demonstrate.

As the leader of your company, how do you cultivate leaders?

Building good to great performing teams has to be one's passion. Once the traits as indicated above are being pursued, there would be several colleagues in the team who would show tremendous resilience to outperform and there would be a few who would show signs of alienation or slow start. It is important to see such green shoots early and ensure that a well designed 'Leadership Development' program is put in place. The delegated work orientation helps leaders to hone their skills on-the-job. Besides, counselling, discussion with leaders in the team including discussions about their aspirations, career path, strengths, and developmental plan, are the key processes adopted towards cultivation of leaders. There is a high involvement of department heads and senior leaders in talent management and succession planning process. A concrete developmental plan is chalked out which is regularly monitored for implementation. We do not stop here, we also discuss our talent at Tata Group level—in which top leaders of the Tata Group engage in developmental discussions, which are recorded for implementation. Besides, each leader is encouraged to announce his target legacies that he or she would like to pursue. This helps leaders undertake initiatives and actions, which help them, achieve good performance.

Can leadership be learnt? In other words, how can a manager become a leader?

Yes, leadership can be learnt and cultivated. Besides natural leaders, a good manager can be groomed to be a good leader through talent management and leadership development process.

What is the role of a professional leader in a promoter-driven company?

The role of a professional leader is no different in a promoter-driven company. A professional leader here should be more conscious of his role to keep his team isolated from the promoters, and guide and steer the team, so that they deliver towards growth of the business so as to create value for all stakeholders.

Since September 2008, the world has fallen into a maelstrom of serial crises. What is the role of a leader in these times?

The true test of a leader is during crises, as to how he motivates and steers the teams through these challenging times. Also, it's important that a leader demonstrates strong ethical values and commitment to clean and transparent governance, so that his team always remains with their head above water.

What has been the biggest leadership challenge you've faced?

As practicing leaders one faces several challenges in their career. For me, change of management at power distribution in Delhi, which was harbinger of corruption, widespread manipulative practices with pathetic customer services and dilapidated infrastructure, to be corrected was one of the big leadership challenge. As one looks back, today the business is profitable with benchmark customer practices and robust infrastructure.

Do you think the role of business leaders has come under cloud —globally and domestically—of late?

There is increasing need for participative and engaging form of leadership. These are challenging times and a lot of commitment and involvement is required to ensure success. I would say even today there are several great business leaders who are leading their companies to success.

Leaders have to often carry the cross of other's wrong doings and inefficiencies, the global banking sector today, for instance. What role can good leadership play to counterbalance this image?

If short-term measures for profitability and vested interests override the fundamental traits, it leads to the kind of issues one has seen in some of the industries. The 'rut to earn' and 'living to earn' are greed that destroy the correct behavior of a leader and must be watched by the key senior stakeholders.

What is your one-line leadership mantra?

Build teams with conviction to perform and thereafter there is nothing impossible.

Who are the leaders that have inspired you?

I am lucky to have worked with a phenomenal leader like Ratan Tata, who has not just inspired me but helped me develop tremendous empathy for human ecosystem and society.

What is the biggest leadership lesson that you have learnt?

Honesty, sincerity, humility and empathy remains one's pride possession and thus should remain integral to one's persona all the time.

What is the best leadership decision you have taken?

To have served large customers and build affectionate teams by accepting the role at Delhi for change management of distribution business.

What is the worst leadership decision you have taken?

Having not promoted an NGO and having launched myself into corporate life.

GAURAV CHOUDHURY

'A leader should lead by example': SAM GHOSH,

GROUP CEO, RELIANCE CAPITAL

Each employee is empowered to think, work and perform like an entrepreneur, says Sam Ghosh, group chief executive officer of Reliance Capital. In an interview, he said that the key role of a leader is to quickly understand new rules and adapt to perform in a new environment. Excerpts:

How do you define a leader?

At an individual level, a leader is a person who helps people grow—in accountability, responsibility, stature and encourages them to lead.

What are the three most important traits of a leader?

A leader should instill confidence in the team, lead by example, and help people realize their potential. I seek a lot of inspiration in the words of Dhirubhai Ambani that said, 'If you can dream it, you can achieve it.'

As a leader of your group, how do you cultivate leaders?

An important trait for any leader is to groom new leaders. 'You are the force' is our motto that sums up our philosophy towards our employees. Each employee is empowered to think, work and perform like an entrepreneur.

Can leadership be learnt? In other words, how can a manager become a leader?

Everyone can become a leader. Good guidance and training are key ingredients for a good leader. A leader must have conviction about the vision and ensure that the team follows.

What is the role of a professional leader in a promoter-driven company?

A professional leader in a promoter-driven company is the most important conduit connecting the promoter's ambition with executable results. On one hand, the professional leader manages the expectations of the promoter, while on the other hand, he or she leads the performance of the team with clear direction to achieve that ambition.

Since September 2008, the world has fallen into a maelstrom of serial crises. What is the role of a leader in these times?

Every crisis changes the environment and impacts the business. It also changes the rules of the game. The key role of the leader is to quickly understand the new rules and adapt to perform in the new environment. You will find different types of leaders during boom times but during tough times, leaders require different traits. What is important for a leader to succeed in all conditions is to learn those different traits.

What has been the biggest leadership challenge you've faced?

Facing the 2008 slowdown and navigating through those times, was the biggest challenge. Overnight, the entire environment changed and we had to evolve ourselves swiftly and steadily. We had to learn, analyse, react, think and rethink every move as it impacted people and business. We also had to keep our teams motivated. It was a great learning as well as the biggest leadership challenge.

Do you think the role of business leaders has come under cloud —globally and domestically—of late?

Domestically, we are still an emerging economy where the businesses, regulators and the consumers are evolving and learning as we grow. The regulators have become customer focused, customers have become more informed and the businesses have become more competitive. This has meant rethinking our priorities in business. The challenge is to maintain high growth.

Leaders have to often carry the cross of other's wrongdoings and inefficiencies, the global banking sector today, for instance. What role can good leadership play to counterbalance this image?

Integrity and customer focus are the key elements to counter these images. The enterprise has to follow the regulations not only in letter but also in spirit.

What is your one-line leadership mantra?

Wealth creation for all stakeholders and leadership in the businesses we operate in.

Who are the global leaders who have inspired you?

I like the management philosophy of Jack Welch. I subscribe to his view that if you pick right people, give them opportunity, delegate authority and compensate them adequately, then your job is almost done.

Who is a leader in the industry whom you respect?

I take a lot of learning and inspiration from Anil D Ambani —especially on how to face challenges undaunted and find opportunity in adversity. If I were to name one company, it would be LIC—a company that I respect immensely. It is a phenomenal company on all counts—trust, brand, reach, products, customer focus and entrepreneurship, among others.

What is the biggest leadership lesson that you have learnt?

When we partnered with Nippon Life Insurance, they asked us about our 50-year plan. We struggled to respond and it changed our approach. Top down, the entire Nippon organization is focused on customer and customer satisfaction. So much so, that in case of the recent tsunami each agent called upon each customer without waiting for them to call, to check their well-being and, wherever applicable, ensure they get the maximum insurance as per their policy. It's remarkable that while the company thinks 50 years ahead, it continues to be the largest private insurer in Japan.

GAURAV CHOUDHURY

'A leader must rebuild strategy as per times': M.G. GEORGE MUTHOOT,

CHAIRMAN, THE MUTHOOT GROUP

George Muthoot, chairman, The Muthoot Group, has more than 55 years of industry experience and is the 3rd generation head of the group. Muthoot shared his best and worst leadership decisions and talks about other leadership issues in an interview. Excerpts:

How do you define a leader?

A leader is someone who influences people towards sustainable achievement of a particular goal. He is someone who provides purpose, direction and motivation while operating to accomplish the mission and improving the efficiency of the team.

What are the three most important traits of a leader?

A true leader has the confidence to stand alone, the courage to make tough decisions and the compassion to listen to the needs of others. He does not set out to be a leader, but becomes one by the equality of his actions and the integrity of his intent. A leader has to be fair and consistent with every individual in his organization and team along with being a great motivator.

As a leader of the Muthoot Group, how do you cultivate leaders?

We constantly communicate our company's core values—ethics, values, reliability, dependability, trustworthiness, goodwill and integrity, to all our team members. As a company, we have always believed that as the organization grows, each team member should also grow. For us (company), our team is our main strength. We consider each team member as a part of the 'Muthoot Family' and not as an employee. The management has always appraised the team member for their hard work, solidarity, cooperation and support in making the organization grow. Infact, we have always advised the team to 'think that you are the owner of the company'.

Can leadership be learnt? In other words, how can a manager become a leader?

Leadership is infused and created by circumstances, but leadership skills can be learnt. It can be acquired, sharpened and improved upon. As a manager, you are focused on managing and sustaining certain things, but as a leader you are expected to enhance those things through coordination, cooperation and contribution of the team.

What is the role of a professional leader in a promoter-driven company?

The foremost role of a professional leader in a promoter-driven company is to be a powerful communicator. He should always re-build his strategy and leadership as per the current time, style and requirements, yet not forgetting his traditional roots and values. He also has to balance the inherent vision of the promoters with that of the larger goals and objectives of all stakeholders.

Since September 2008, the world has fallen into a maelstrom of serial crises. What is the role of a leader in these times?

I believe that failure to respond to a crisis is a failure of leadership. A leader will always take a crisis situation in a positive spirit, as a crisis is a time for him to prove his mettle and set examples for others. As the saying goes 'When the going gets tough, the tough get going.' Crisis is a time when the leader takes tough decisions and travels the path less traversed. It's important that a leader demonstrates strong ethical values and commitment during such situations. We have seen our leaders taking tough decisions and re-emphasizing the core values we believe in during difficult situations. That is why our organization takes great pride in our history of having 126 years of unblemished track record.

What has been the biggest leadership challenge you've faced?

'To work within the varied expectations of a team' has always been the biggest challenge every leader faces. In today's competitive scenario this challenge has further enhanced itself, as individual growth is overpowering the collective/corporate growth.

Do you think the role of business leaders has come under cloud —globally and domestically—of late?

The growing effect of globalization has presented new challenges as well as distorted the old. New challenges of sustainable development and corporate governance, mixed with the distortion of fundamental issues such as ethics and values has presented opportunities to distiguish good leaders from the bad. There are leaders who despite challenging times have maintained their ethics, values, integrity and led their organization towards success, albeit a bit slower. Unfortunately, these intrinsic values never show up on a corporate report while evaluating performance.

Leaders have to often carry the cross of other's wrongdoings and inefficiencies, the global banking sector today, for instance. What role can good leadership play to counterbalance this image?

A leader is as good as the weakest person in the team. His strength is effectively gauged from the ability of the weakest member. As a leader, one is responsible on different levels while achieving the desired results and should be ready to own the responsibilities of his team as much as he is willing to take the credit for their perfomance.

What would be your one-line leadership mantra?

Rise to the occasion and perform the best you can.

Who are the leaders that have inspired you?

Everyone has a person they consider to be their role-model. A person who inspires them in a deep and profound manner. My inspiration came from my father who still remains my ultimate role model.

What is the biggest leadership lesson that you have learnt?

The biggest leadership lesson I have learnt is to never forgo your ethics, values, reliability, dependability, trustworthiness, goodwill and integrity in any situation. Every situation, good or bad, is a learning experience.

What is the best leadership decision you have taken?

The best leadership decisions I have taken are the ones where I don't take any (active decision) and allow my team to come to their own logical conclusion as to what is best for all stakeholders. I understand my role to be that of an enabler and not one of a solution provider.

GAURAV CHOUDHURY

'Vision, integrity and empathy are critical': VINCENT COBEE,

GLOBAL HEAD DATSUN BRAND AND
CORPORATE VICE-PRESIDENT,
NISSAN MOTOR CO. LTD

Vincent Cobee, global head Datsun brand and corporate vice-president of Japanese automaker Nissan Motor, recently revitalized the Datsun brand that seeks to manufacture affordable cars in developing markets like India, Russia, Indonesia and South Africa. Datsun's global journey begins early next year in India with its small car, Go, and the brand is expected to account as much as a third of Nissan's global sales in times to come. In an interview, Cobee said that a leader's emotional quotient should be as high as his intellectual quotient. Excerpts:

How do you define a leader? What does leadership mean for you?

I would define a leader as someone who is able to steer a group of people with multiple directions and mandates. It is very important for a leader to possess a bird's eye view of all perspectives. This is particularly important during times of crisis and uncertainty.

What are the three most important traits of a leader?

I would consider the elements of vision, integrity and empathy as most critical for any leader. Vision as mentioned earlier is necessary to keep in mind the long-term goals and vision of the team and the organization at large. Impediments may come as short-term hiccups, so a broad, long-term vision and the ability to keep the focus on track is necessary. Integrity is absolute. A person who is accountable with unimpeachable integrity is the best worker. Despite errors and mistakes, I would depend on a person who speaks the truth and would deliver the same to all my colleagues and team members. Finally, empathy because as a leader one should also keep in mind that we are after all dealing with complex human beings. An emotional quotient as high as an intellectual quotient and empathy for people's difficulties are paramount.

As the head of a company that is being revived, how do you cultivate leaders?

I was myself cultivated and nurtured by seniors. I was given opportunities to take on more; tougher and bigger projects. I believe that if you provide opportunities and delegate to trusted people with potential and ambition, they automatically rise to the challenges they are presented and mould themselves as leaders. We can meanwhile coach and support them behind the scenes, so that they succeed and learn on what they have begun.

Can leadership be learnt? In other words, how can a manager become a leader?

Leadership can be learned, but through strong mentoring and attempting increasing difficult challenges and by succeeding in those challenges. A manager attempts any assignment from a management point of view, but a leader is the outcome of the assignment if it is successful. Success is a measurement of a leader on whether he is able to grow with others and by taking them along for the success they enjoy together.

What is the role of a leader in times like these when the macroeconomic indicators are uncertain?

During uncertain times, a leader must be aware of the risks and perils of doing business. Growth cannot be the only indicator for all business processes. One must be clear about the objectives and the main values—accept, and communicate about the uncertainties; do contingency planning and most importantly, stay calm during the uncertainty.

Do you think the role of business leaders has come under a cloud globally of late?

No. Maybe, the proportion of real leaders is decreasing due to the professionalization of business. Also, the public and media are more interested in numbers and economic failures than in human factors and leadership traits of people. Business leaders cannot be held responsible for all failures, though they can be held accountable for their strategic and tactical decisions alone. The global environment and interconnectedness of the world has a lot to do with the way business is conducted around the world and this also has a bearing in why companies succeed and fail, particularly for a business which is transnational.

Leaders have to often carry the cross of other's wrongdoings and inefficiencies, the global banking sector today, for instance. What role can good leadership play to counterbalance this image?

As a leader, one must endeavour and ensure that public trust in private enterprise is maintained. Private enterprise remains one of the key engines for economic growth and public trust in the sanctity and efficacy of private enterprise must be held intact.

What is your one line leadership mantra?

Ask for forgiveness, not for permission.

SUMANT BANERJI

'A leader should keep his head in the clouds, but feet on the ground': VIJAY THADANI,

CEO AND CO-FOUNDER, NIIT LIMITED

Vijay K. Thadani, chief executive officer of NIIT Ltd, a global talent development corporation, shares his leadership mantra in an interview and discusses a range of issues on leadership. Excerpts:

How do you define a leader?

A leader is an inspiring mentor whom others would want to follow.

What are the three most important traits of a leader?

Leaders should be strategic thinkers, who inspire others with their vision. They should have the courage to take bold decisions and lead from the front. They should have the confidence to hire people better than themselves and promote risk taking.

As a leader of the NIIT group, how do you cultivate leaders?

We start by enrolling people in NIIT's vision, values and beliefs. From there, we help them build their own aspiration and career path. We give them challenging goals and encourage making mistakes as long as it contributes to their learning. We engage them in cross disciplinary teams, such as in our chairman's 'Quality Club' program, we provide lateral movement opportunities and finally we have formal leadership certification programs. This creates a pipeline of high calibre leaders aligned to NIIT's vision and values, for effective organization building.

What is the role of a professional leader in a promoter-driven company?

The terminology, promoter-driven, is more suited to the industrial age. In an organization of the knowledge economy such as ours, 'professional founders' would be a more appropriate terminology. The role of the leader remains the same i.e. to inspire with thoughts and lead by action. The owner-employee relationship is also redundant. In fact, at NIIT, we have banned the term 'employee'. We call ourselves 'NIITians', a term which creates a common alignment of equal stakes in the emotional ownership of the organization.

Since September 2008, the world has fallen into a maelstrom of serial crises. What is the role of a leader in these times?

Good weather never made good sailors. As an organization with 32 years of experience, with both good and not so good times, we have seen that successful leaders in times of crisis re-emphasize the values and beliefs of the organization. They make courageous moves because they see crisis as an opportunity for them, to learn and prove their mettle.

What has been the biggest leadership challenge you've faced?

In the late 90's we were backing internet technologies and in 2001 the dot-com bubble burst. It was a wakeup call for revisiting our strategy set. We realized that in short-term, we would need to cut costs. The NIIT value system got exemplified with NIITians coming forward to take a voluntary pay cut rather than downsize the organization. So, in many ways this crisis tested the tenacity of this organization and strengthened our core belief that NIIT is about its people.

Do you think the role of business leaders has come under cloud —globally and domestically—of late?

Just as leaders get accolades when their teams and organizations do well, they also get the flak when it is otherwise. The global and Indian economy is volatile and business formulae in some of the sectors such as IT are changing. In times like this, when organizations struggle to find their S curves back, the role of a business leader does come under cloud. For great leaders, this is an opportunity.

Leaders have to often carry the cross of other's wrong doings and inefficiencies, the global banking sector today, for instance. What role can good leadership play to counterbalance this image?

Being a leader is not about maintaining an image. It is about being driven by a vision, a cause. When leaders inherit a role, they have to accept all the baggage that comes with it. When they completely own the challenge, is when their turnaround success story begins.

What is your one line leadership mantra?

Your growth is the derivative of the growth of each member of your team.

Who are the leaders that have inspired you?

I was fortunate to be born in times of great change, where I could see the contributions of many great social, literary and scientific leaders. I had the opportunity to be inspired by someone nearly every day. Even in my organization, every now and then I discover a new trait of leadership that becomes my inspiration for the day.

Who is a leader in your industry that you respect?

Of the many that I hold in very high esteem, I have the highest respect for F.C. Kohli, the father of the Indian software industry.

What is the biggest leadership lesson that you have learnt?

Leaders should always keep their heads in the cloud but feet firmly planted on the ground.

What is the best leadership decision you have taken?

The best decision was to maintain a single identity for NIIT through our values and beliefs framework. Even when we transcended continents, products and business strategies, our values and beliefs framework is the bond that binds all NIITians together.

What is the worst leadership decision you have taken?

For the first 15 years, we thrived on innovation. However, as the scale grew, we felt the need to introduce a strong quality and process orientation. It was a very successful movement, but somewhere we lost the balance between process and innovation. In the last few years, we made course correction and introduced a series of innovative learning solutions, with NIIT Cloud Campus being the most recent.

GAURAV CHOUDHURY

'Growing as a leader is a learning process': ARUP ROY CHOUDHURY,

CHAIRMAN & MD, NTPC LTD

Arup Roy Choudhury is the chairman and managing director of India's largest and one of the world's best power companies, NTPC Ltd. He has the distinction of becoming the youngest CEO of a Central Public Sector Enterprise (CPSE) at the age of 44 when he joined as CMD, National Buildings Construction Corporation Ltd (NBCC) in 2001. His vision and leadership transformed NBCC from a sick company with negative net worth and salary back log in 2001, into a blue-chip enterprise. In an interview, he said that a leader aligns the personal goals of each individual in his team to the corporate or group goal and assigns measurable and achievable milestones and gets them evaluated against predefined targets. Edited excerpts:

How do you define a leader?

A leader has to be a visionary. There are hordes of people who can see the next, that is, the second milestone but a leader would be able to see the milestone beyond that and see right through to the destination.

As a leader of your group, how do you cultivate leaders?

A leader aligns the personal goals of each individual in his team to the corporate or group goal and assigns measurable and achievable milestones and gets them evaluated against predefined targets. In order to groom leaders, it is important to tell the executives that they have been selected and not elected. Otherwise, they would lose clarity and focus in decision-making.

Can leadership be learnt? How can a manager be a leader?

Leadership has to be learnt. It is not part of one's genetic code. Otherwise, we would have children of all corporate leaders as good business leaders. If you look around, you will notice many family-driven companies have disintegrated by the time the third generation took over the mantle. It is true that if one has some genetic traits or character traits which go with leadership roles, it is easier for these individuals to adapt to a leadership role. But growing as a leader is a continuous learning process and one has to keep all senses open.

What is the role of a professional leader in a government-promoted company?

Government-promoted companies are run by excellent professional leaders and, in fact, many private companies are run by business leaders who have joined them from the government fold. The role of a professional leader in a government company is to demonstrate that it is possible to acquire business excellence and competitiveness while complying with the elaborate set of norms and rules under which they perform. In a government company you cannot lay people off and so it is important to get the best out of everyone in the team with an effective strategy customized for each team member.

What has been the biggest leadership challenge you've faced?

The biggest leadership challenge was when I was made CEO of an organization which had not been paying salaries for over six months, had nine unions to foment trouble among already disgruntled groups of employees. It was a government company so it was also not possible to give any pink slips or layoff any people. To lead it into making it a profitable and dividend-paying listed company was the biggest challenge.

ANUPAMA AIRY

'A leader knows how to build, nurture a team': KAPIL CHOPRA,

PRESIDENT, OBEROI GROUP

As the president of the Oberoi Group, Kapil Chopra is responsible for all Oberoi and Trident hotels in India. An alumnus of The Oberoi Centre of Learning and Development (OCLD), Chopra's experience as an hotelier spans over two decades. He has been instrumental in opening of properties such as The Oberoi, Dubai, The Oberoi and Trident, Gurgaon, and recently, Trident, Hyderabad. In an interview, he said that a leader should be an agent of change. Excerpts:

How do you define a leader and what are the three most important traits of a leader?

A leader is someone who leads by example and believes in building and nurturing his team. The three traits are: team-building—the ability to work in teams and inspire them; intensity of purpose; and business acumen.

As a leader of the group, how do you cultivate leaders?

I think the first thing is to ensure that there is transparency in the system. The second thing for people to remember is a line that I often use, 'learn to fail fast'. So if you really haven't failed at any given time, then you haven't ever pushed yourself to achieve the best that you can. It is always important for leaders to have a business and strategic orientation. When you go to work every day, you have to ask yourself a question, best summed up in one of the Ten Commandments from Hewlett Packard—contribute everyday.

Can leadership be learnt? In other words, how can a manager become a leader?

Yes, leadership can be learnt. Leadership traits can be imbibed. A manager takes instructions and implements them, but a leader charts the path and energizes his team.

What is your one line leadership mantra?

'Whatever it takes' it is a liberating line, which puts the onus of performance on the individual and not on the circumstances surrounding a situation.

What has been the biggest leadership challenge you've faced?

One of the biggest leadership challenges that I have faced is the opening of The Oberoi, Gurgaon. Trident, Gurgaon, had the highest revenue per available room for any hotel in India and is an iconic hotel in Gurgaon from every single standpoint and played host to top global boards from across the world. Opening The Oberoi, Gurgaon, just adjacent to Trident, and that too when the global economy had not completely recovered, was a real challenge. We opened in the summer of 2011—traditionally the worst time to open a luxury hotel as you are approaching the low season. We also opened with a premium of Rs 4,000 per room as compared to the Trident and with the highest average room rate for any hotel in India. The whole idea was to still deliver value at a higher price point so that guests appreciate the value they are getting and not perceive the hotel to be expensive. That was one moment when I felt we might have overextended ourselves. At The Oberoi, Gurgaon, we raised the bar for city hotels in India. It was a big leap of faith in creating a world-class hotel.

Who are the leaders who have inspired you?

Sachin Tendulkar because for me he epitomizes competence across the board. Michael Dell because he redefined how computers were sold—personalized to your requirement. Dr Devi Shetty because he revolutionized heart care because he believed that Rs 10 per family member per month should be enough to provide quality health care. My father, Dr Chopra, because he taught me that it is more important to contribute to the society you live in than focus on material gains.

Who is a leader in your industry whom you respect?

Undoubtedly, PRS Oberoi, executive chairman of the Oberoi Group—a legendary hotelier and a role model for all of us. His enthusiasm, passion and zeal for service excellence are beyond anything that I have ever seen.

If you were asked to give one advice to other business leaders in India, what would that be?

I would just request everyone to be a change agent. We are all fortunate but then, there are issues in our country that need help. It is important that business leaders contribute to society in a significant way; writing a small cheque every year is not enough. Believing in a cause, committing personal time and money to improve the lives of people around us or contributing whether in education, sanitation or healthcare for the economically weaker sections of society is the minimum we can do.

ANUPAMA AIRY AND MAHUA VENKATESH

'Leadership is doing the right things': RASHESH SHAH,

CHAIRMAN & CEO, EDELWEISS GROUP

Rashesh Shah, chairman and CEO of the Edelweiss Group, has been in the Indian financial services sector for over 20 years. Before Edelweiss, he worked with ICICI, then India's premier industrial development bank and today its largest private sector bank. Shah founded Edelweiss in 1996 with equity capital of R1 crore. His focus on innovation and passion for growth through expansion have been a key differentiator for Edelweiss, helping it combine growth-oriented entrepreneurship with a strong focus on risk. Excerpts from an interview:

How do you define a leader?

A leader is someone who has a vision, is capable of inspiring others so that this vision becomes a common goal, and is able to get them to work as a team, to achieve things that would be out of reach if they worked individually.

As the leader of your company, how do you cultivate leaders?

We have a well-defined, multi-layered programme of identifying and cultivating leaders from the early stages of their career. Once identified, they are empowered. There is constant communication with this group to encourage them to think and act one or two levels above their pay grade, which helps them reframe perceptions about potential, and gets them to think like a CEO. The results are astonishing.

Can leadership be learnt? How can a manager become a leader?

Some qualities of a leader are innate; for instance, a sense of values and integrity. But beyond this, leadership can be learnt and has, in fact, been learnt through the ages. Just think of the way professional armies have trained their leaders. Being a good manager is a necessary starting point, but to be a leader you need to learn new skills and make a transition. There are many facets to this. You need to graduate from being a specialist to a generalist. You also need to be able to integrate the collective knowledge of cross-functional teams, and make appropriate trade-offs to solve complex organizational problems. Managers can afford to focus on tactics but to become leaders they need to learn to strategize, look at the larger picture, figure out patterns and anticipate the influence of external factors.

What is the role of a professional leader in a promoter-driven company?

'Promoter-driven companies' are a peculiarly Asian concept, where the founders continue to hold sway over management decisions by the fact that they promoted the company. In the West, especially in the US, ownership and leadership are generally divorced. When the goals of the promoters and professional leaders are in alignment, it has produced near miraculous results. In these cases, the role of a 'professional' leader is no different from what it would be otherwise—growing the business in the most profitable manner so as to create value for all stakeholders. However if the goals of the promoters and other stakeholders diverge, it puts a lot of pressure on the 'professional' leaders, who then have to perform a high-wire act, needing a lot of skill and tact.

Since September 2008, the world has fallen into a maelstrom of crises. What is the role of a leader in these times?

The true test of a leader—be that of a company or a country—is how he or she deals with crises. If we look at great leaders in history, a few common themes emerge. It starts with recognizing that there is a crisis and then goes on to understanding the root causes. The next step is to recognize how bad things are, and if they could get worse. To paraphrase Peter Drucker, leadership is not just doing things right, but doing the right things, demonstrably and repeatedly. A leader must build trust, the key to tackling any crisis. One adage that we have always followed: 'Never waste a good crisis'. Every crisis has the seeds of an opportunity.

What has been the biggest leadership challenge you have faced?

The two biggest challenges for any organization are scaling up, and then to reorient it once it has gathered scale. For us the initial challenge was to get potential employees and investors to believe in our idea that India needed new-age diversified financial services providers—which we wanted Edelweiss to be. The second big challenge was our expansion from being capital market centric, diversifying it into adjacent spaces such as credit, commodities, housing finance and life insurance.

What is your one line leadership mantra?

To quote former US Secretary of State Henry Kissinger, 'The task of a leader is to take his people from where they are to where they haven't been.'

What is your best leadership decision?

We have always set our goals and aspirations very high and have made sure we never lost focus of these because of short term challenges.

And the worst?

With the benefit of hindsight, I realize that our timing on a few decisions may not be perfect. For example, perhaps we were early with our IPO. We were in the process of building new businesses and looking back, I now feel it would have made more sense to approach the markets a couple of years later.

GAURAV CHOUDHURY

'A leader needs to laugh at failure': KISHORE BIYANI,

FOUNDER AND PROMOTER, FUTURE GROUP

After more than 25 years in manufacturing, marketing, and retailing of ready-made garments, the founder and promoter of the Future Group, Kishore Biyani, is preparing himself for a second innings. Born in a middle-class trading family and credited for introducing modern retail in India, Biyani chose to dream big and take risks even as others viewed his ideas with scepticism. Biyani spoke about why failure is important, and how he has groomed everyone in his company to laugh at failures. Excerpts from an interview:

What does leadership mean to you?

Leadership is all about taking decisions. It is about how you build teams, achieve fruitful outcomes, deliver and execute while taking people along and also about creating positive attitude and removing negative energy.

Can leadership be nurtured?

While some are born leaders, in many instances leadership can be developed. Overall, there are two kinds of leaders—the thinking ones, and the skilled ones. Thought leadership is ingrained, while the other is acquired. Thought leaders are born. At 25 years of age, one cannot suddenly turn into a thought leader as by then thought is developed. But one can develop skills anytime.

Who are your role models?

One can have a role model in every discipline of life. On the supply chain side for instance, Victor Fung (group chairman of Li & Fung) is my role model. I see him as a thought leader. The first time I read one of his articles was 20 years ago in Harvard Business Review, where he was a regular contributor. For retail, Sam Walton (an American businessman best known for founding the retailers Walmart and Sam's Club) is our role model at the Future Group. When it comes to entrepreneurship, all of us grew up with Dhirubhai Ambani (founder of Reliance Industries) as a role model and he is still an inspiration for what he achieved and the way he overcame challenges. At a personal level, I find Anil Agarwal (founder and executive chairman of the UK-based Vedanta Resources Corporation) fascinating in terms of his vision and his ability to take big decisions.

What are your strengths?

All of us have both positives and negatives. If you look at it from the retail point of view, to give an example, a good retailer has to be strong on every point. I cannot claim that I am strong in all areas. I believe a strong leader is the one who recognizes one's weaknesses and flaws and finds people to fill in those areas.

What are your weaknesses?

We have too many weaknesses. For instance, an ambition to do a lot of things and achieve too much…

What are these weaknesses? Is supply chain a weakness?

Supply chain was never a weakness for us. We have always been the best and we are keeping apace of remaining the best. We can be better on the capital side, though inflow of foreign funds is no longer a worry. Even the best-laid plans do not fall in place at times.

Are failures stepping-stones to success?

One cannot achieve much without failures. The only ones who make no mistakes are the ones who sleep. I think we know how to learn from failures and have learnt to laugh at them. We are perhaps the only company in India that has acknowledged failure. We have trained everyone to admit failure because until one admits failure, he is unable to change. The first thing is to defend, then escape and pass on the blame. I have never blamed anyone for my mistakes. The leader has to take the blame.

After Independence, has India nurtured enough leaders?

India still lags in this area. We are somewhat weak in thought leadership. We have been under foreign rule for so many centuries, and that has affected our thought leadership, our ability to believe in ourselves and pursue our own ideas. We are still 'not there' when it comes to product innovation. Nevertheless, we are at a stage where we are building the nation. India is transforming, and fast. You will see more thought leaders, who are innovators, emerge.

Has your leadership style changed over the years?

At every stage in life, one learns and matures and sees new scenarios, new opportunities and new possibilities. In a fast growing economy, one focusses on growing revenues, exploring new businesses. In a subdued economy, growth has to be multidimensional—growth could mean growing efficiencies, growing margins and getting more from the same. Even today, we are just as ambitious, but our ambition is more about getting more from the same scale of business or operations or resources through better productivity and better execution.

You have built your retail empire from scratch. What do you think will be the challenges for the next generation?

The pace of change is increasing every day—there are new trends, new technologies and often contra-trends as well. Each of these brings new challenges and opportunities—depending upon how innovative and agile one is. For leaders of tomorrow, coping with change, and even benefiting from it, will be the biggest challenge. First generation entrepreneurs start with almost nothing and therefore have little fear of failure. As business grows, achievements, success and scale come in, and then people often fear losing these. That affects fresh thoughts and innovation in the enterprise. Second-generation entrepreneurs, who can overcome this and pursue new ideas, and not just act as preservers of an enterprise, will create a name for themselves.

RACHIT VATS

'Empower people to make mistakes': VSEVOLOD ROZANOV,

PRESIDENT AND CEO, MTS INDIA

Vsevolod Rozanov, president and CEO, MTS India, the mobile telecom service brand of Sistema Shyam TeleServices Ltd. He spoke about the challenges he faced after coming to India and a range of issues covering leadership and management. Excerpts from an interview:

How do you define a leader?

I think a leader is someone who has a vision, takes responsibility for execution, executes it, and cares about people and team spirit. He also inspires and unites the team for a cause. The most important thing for me is responsibility. Someone without a vision can't be a leader.

What are the most important traits of a leader?

The important traits that a leader should have are vision, taking responsibility for execution and uniting the team for execution.

As the leader of SSTL in India, how do you cultivate leaders?

I think here the question lies in empowering the people to make mistakes and accept those mistakes. Unfortunately, in a developing world we have much more hierarchy and often feel shy to speak-up, to accelerate the issues, to share the ideas and look up to the boss to charter the way, and then execute. If you think that there is a good person then accordingly give him responsibility, few ownerships and let him take the responsibility for execution.

Can leadership be learnt? Or how can a manager become a leader?

I think there should be some internal flame or some purpose to drive mobility inside a person. What is critical for a person is not just to develop but also seek opportunity to develop. A person can do a lot by attentive observing. Of course, the leadership of the group has responsibility for developing successive leaders.

What is the role of a professional leader in a promoter-driven company?

How different is Russia from India? I think in many companies, Russia is no different from India, promoters are leaders also. This could be a good thing or a bad thing. In some cases, some leaders cannot tolerate other leaders. At the end of the day, one person cannot do everything. Business is not led by just one leader but a collection of leaders. Even creating an atmosphere for thousands of executors will not work unless it is considered a natural monopoly, which ultimately leads to exploring some resource. In fact, let me be a little provocative: professional managers are also responsible for protecting promoters from themselves. Because, even if professional managers have pulse and new ideas to do something good, in reality the role of the professional managers is to engage the promoters into discussion and create a framework that basically helps the organization to follow the course charter by promoters to manage the associated resources.

What has been the biggest leadership challenge you've faced?

The biggest challenge that I faced was landing in India in July 2008, leading a team of 10 people.

Is India that bad that it became a challenge for you?

It is not India which is bad. India is a great country because it provides challenges. It was a personal challenge for me. Before that, I had an experience as chief operating officer (COO), chief financial officer (CFO), etc., but here I was given a task to not just create a company, but to create a company and a brand with significant presence on almost complete white paper from the scratch.

What is your leadership mantra?

My mantra is based on a famous Russian saying 'Per aspera ad astra', when translated in English can be best explained as 'through hardships to the stars'.

Who are the leaders that have inspired you?

I personally admire three leaders who have noticing personalities because they had achieved some interesting things through their leadership qualities. Sergei Korolev, a famous chief designer of Russian space programme, Lee Kwan Yew, the founder of modern Singapore and a true statesman, and Mikhail Kutuzov, a Field Marshal of the Russia who won the war against Napoleon.

What is the best leadership decision you have taken?

I believe I am yet to take the best leadership decision. I have made good decisions but the best is yet to come.

What is the worst leadership decision you have taken?

One decision I can confess, which I really regret for not taking much earlier. Our biggest achievement as I mentioned earlier is clear establishment of brand in very short span of time in very competitive market. Our service basically focuses on data. Looking back, we should have started our data business right from day one. We started business one year after the launch. It took us another 6–8 more months to learn how to do things right.

Is that a lesson learnt or is that a decision that you should have taken earlier?

These are two sides of one thing. I should have been more thoughtful about the opportunities and should have been able to take the decision and make it faster.

GAURAV CHOUDHURY

'Leaders must drive inclusive behaviour': ARI SARKER,

DIVISION PRESIDENT, SOUTH ASIA, MASTERCARD

A ri Sarker, the South Asia division president of MasterCard, says real life challenges and adversities when dealt with courage and fortitude are more easily identifiable at an individual level and therefore more inspiring. In an interview, Sarker said that leadership is an acquired skill, and any leadership-building journey starts with the value system of an individual passed on by parents or elders as a child. Excerpts:

How do you define a leader?

If I were to hazard a definition, at the cost of being simplistic, it would be: a leader is someone who inspires and motivates a team to achieve extraordinary results.

What are the three most important traits of a leader?

Leadership is situational with many facets to it; nevertheless, there are some basic tenets that one should adhere to, and the top three for me would be the following: be real and authentic, inspire others and be inclusive.

As a leader of MasterCard, how do you cultivate leaders?

Leadership development is a continuous process for any individual, but it is also important to recognize that you can be a leader leading a team and be a leader as an individual contributor who does not manage teams directly under oneself but has to influence many diverse stakeholders. My specific style of cultivating leaders is by reinforcing leadership traits that an individual should build by sharing real life stories on what builds great leaders. Real life challenges and adversities when dealt with courage and fortitude are more easily identifiable at an individual level and therefore more inspiring.

Can leadership be learnt? In other words, how can a manager become a leader?

Leadership is an acquired skill, and any leadership-building journey starts with the value system of an individual passed on by parents or elders as a child. A manager earns his leadership credentials if he or she is able to inspire others, appreciate and encourage differing points of view and drive focus and execution to a common goal at the same time. Leaders need to demonstrate flexibility and drive inclusive behaviour, yet be firm and disciplined in executing the agreed agenda.

What has been the biggest leadership challenge you've faced?

I moved into a role that had a dysfunctional team, coterie culture, mistrust among colleagues, and low morale with attrition rate at

28% in the team. The biggest challenge was working through all of the above and driving change felt like changing the wheels of a running car. But, when I look back at that experience, it was tough but extremely satisfying given how much the needle had moved over a 12-month period.

Do you think the role of business leaders has come under a cloud both globally and domestically of late?

I don't believe business leaders have come under a cloud of late. What is clear is that leadership roles have become more challenging given the environment we live in today—fast pace of change, much greater ambiguity and uncertainty in the external environment, technology and speed of communication, all shortening the reaction time for any leader. These, coupled with the public scrutiny they are subjected to make them far more vulnerable and be judged more often than before.

Leaders have to often carry the cross of other's wrongdoings and inefficiencies, the global banking sector today, for instance. What role can good leadership play to counterbalance this image?

It is all about leadership to erase a tainted past and restore confidence in the larger system. The global financial crisis created a complete collapse of confidence that was far more damaging then the dollars lost (although that too was very significant and damaging). Therefore, restoring confidence with honest and trusting leadership and be seen to be acting decisively to address the challenges by doing as promised go a long way to rebuild the trust deficit.

What is your one line leadership mantra?

Leadership is not a popularity contest… Just keep it REAL! And be FAIR!

What is the best leadership decision you have taken?

The best leadership decision I took was in 2003 when I decided to become an entrepreneur for an 18-month period. This period was one of the most testing leadership experiences for me but one of the most enriching from a self-development standpoint.

What is the worst leadership decision you have taken?

Replacing a member of my team in haste only to discover the challenge was somewhere else. This has made me go deeper in my own evaluation of people.

GAURAV CHOUDHURY

'A leader should be courageous, honest, fair': MELT VAN DER SPUY,

MANAGING DIRECTOR, ELI LILLY AND COMPANY (INDIA) PVT. LTD

Melt Van Der Spuy, managing director, Eli Lilly and Company (India) Pvt. Ltd, the 10th largest pharmaceutical company in the world, joined the firm 18 years ago as a sales representative. He was has appointed as the MD of Indian Operations in 2011. Spuy says that leadership can be learnt and shares his leadership mantra. Excerpts from an interview:

How do you define a leader?

A leader can be described as an individual who is capable of aligning a group of people to a commonly identified cause with tremendous passion and commitment—and as a result brings about an extraordinary result. The leader must have the ability to connect to the heart of the people that he/she will be leading.

What are the three most important traits of a leader?

To be courageous: there are many things you can learn in solitude but courage is not one of them. To be honest and act with integrity: yes means yes, no means no. To be fair and consistent with every individual in your organization: there are no favourites.

In your own company, how do you cultivate leaders?

We have various processes to help us effectively recruit, assess and develop people with leadership capabilities. The best way to develop leaders is not by classroom training sessions on leadership but by giving them challenging assignments. Abigail Adams was right when she counseled her son John Quincy that 'hard times are the crucible in which character and leadership are forged.'

Can leadership be learnt?

Yes. Character forms a critical part of leadership. Many leaders fail as a result of character issues. The building blocks of character are virtues such as prudence (be wise) and fortitude (be courageous) to name but a few. Human beings are not born with these virtues but they are to be developed through the attainment of knowledge, difficult life experiences and having the right mentors to help guide our development.

Since 2008 the world has fallen into a maelstrom of serial crises. What is the role of a leader in these times?

In these challenging times, the role of the leader is more critical than ever before. Many people have lost their faith in leadership due to the many public examples of personal failures of leaders. As leaders, we have the responsibility to fulfill our roles with excellence and integrity. We also know that no matter how tough the market is that we are working in there will always be winners and losers. It is also important as leaders that we don't quit in the challenging times—there is an African proverb that says, 'calm seas don't make skillful sailors!' It is almost always in these challenging times that we learn most about ourselves as leaders and as a result grow has human beings and our ability to lead.

Do you think the role of business leaders has come under cloud —globally and domestic—of late?

Yes. There are too many examples where leaders have failed the people that they serve. The primary safeguard against corruption and financial disaster is not tighter controls but making sure we recruit, develop and appoint people of integrity into leadership positions. Most malpractices don't happen as a result of ignorance to the laws that govern a country or a specific industry—they happen as a result of a leader's failure in judgment and character. It is important as we develop people that we look into the continuous development of key virtues that will form their character. There is simply no substitute for a solid character.

Leaders have to often carry the cross of other's wrongdoings and inefficiencies, the global banking sector today, for instance. What role can good leadership play to counterbalance this image?

Within your own organization you are responsible for every person you appoint into a leadership position. This is one of our most critical task as a leaders and one where our success rates needs to improve dramatically. We don't always control what happens in our environment but we have significant control over who we appoint as leaders. Reality is that in every market no matter how tough—there are always winners and losers. Appoint the right leaders and you are much more likely to be a winner!

What is your one line leadership mantra?

Top results with integrity! It is not only 'what' we achieve but 'how' we achieve it. I believe that as leaders we need to spend an equal amount of time discussing and reviewing both the 'what' and 'how' of the result.

Who are the leaders that have inspired you?

Nelson Mandela—political prisoner jailed for 27 years—reconciled South Africans and ensured peaceful first ever multiracial elections. Theodore Roosevelt—Thomas Marshall, the US vice-president said, 'Death had to take Roosevelt sleeping, for if he had been awake, there would have been a fight.'

What is the biggest leadership lesson that you have learnt?

Captured in the famous words of Harry Truman, 'You can accomplish anything in life, provided that you do not mind who gets the credit.' I think we have all met people that are more concerned about keeping their boss informed about their great accomplishments than recognizing the people below them that got the job done. The leader needs to make sure the right people are appropriately recognized for their efforts.

What are the best and worst leadership decisions you have taken?

Early on in my career there were a few cases when I waited too long to make a people-related change in a critical role. As I learned from these experiences early on, it has helped me in more recent roles to act quickly where it was needed and as a result bring about positive results.

'A true leader always walks the talk': BANMALI AGRAWALA,

PRESIDENT & CEO, GE SOUTH ASIA

Banmali Agrawala is the president and CEO for GE South Asia and is responsible for all of GE's operations in the region. A veteran in the energy domain, Agrawala has over 29 years of global experience. He has served in several senior leadership roles in the Wartsila Group and in the Tata Power Group. He said that one never stops learning at GE. Excerpts from an interview:

How do you define a leader?

Leadership is all about being oneself, it's that simple and that difficult. It is also about making others perform better in your presence and for that behaviour to continue even after you are gone. For me, it is about having clarity and honesty of purpose, putting others before the self and possessing the willingness to be led.

You have recently taken over as the head in India. How is the experience and what are the challenges?

To be responsible for GE in the India and South Asia region is a great opportunity and responsibility. To have the ability to make a difference on such a scale is an exhilarating feeling and that's precisely why 'GE is in India for India'. GE is also a 130-year-old treasure. This treasure has to be handled with care.

Can leadership be learnt? In other words, how can a manager become a leader?

Leadership can certainly be learnt provided the attitude is right. Skills can be acquired but attitude is something that gets shaped very early and is difficult to change later. One just has to keep performing to the best of one's ability in the current role without thinking of the 'next step'. Leadership is a lot about judgement as almost every issue that comes up is 'grey' and judgement is needed to make the right choices. Judgement in turn comes from experience and from going through uncomfortable situations. Getting comfortable with ambiguity and uncertainty and not being disheartened by failure are an important part of the learning process which, again comes largely through exposure. GE offers leadership programmes that are designed to build the next generation of leaders.

What is your one line leadership mantra?

Walk the talk.

Who are the leaders who have inspired you?

Ratan Tata and Jeff Immelt are the two leaders who have always inspired me. Ratan Tata for his decency and character which also defines the Tata Group and Jeff for his strategic thinking, clarity of communication and decisive actions.

How difficult is it to lead a company that has interests in several divergent fields?

GE is in divergent fields but the overall theme is 'industrial and infrastructure'. Being a conglomerate does help in a volatile environment; besides, for a company of the size of GE, it also provides the ability to provide wholesome development to regions/countries and other large corporates. From an employee's perspective, the diversity provides tremendous opportunity for leadership development. The difficult part is to get all 'cylinders' firing at the same time consistently. Overall, being a conglomerate is a huge advantage.

How do you motivate your team at a time when the economy is in a slowdown mode and sentiments are at its lowest?

The GE portfolio being so diverse and global, there are always opportunities for employees. Many businesses still have opportunity to grow in the Indian region even in this downturn. Further, sourcing from India has become even more attractive than earlier. In GE, the emphasis and investment on people and technology development is maintained irrespective of the economic environment. There cannot be a better place to be than GE in such volatile times. GE employees have a strong sense of bonding and ownership with the brand.

How do you manage to nurture that culture?

The culture of GE is derived from its values. The deep commitment to ethics, technology, meritocracy, transparency and respect for each other is practiced by every GE employee. I can say with great confidence that one never stops learning at GE. My job is to ensure that these values are never compromised no matter what the provocation.

ANUPAMA AIRY

'A leader must be unbiased and patient': JYOTSNA SURI,

CMD, THE LALIT SURI HOSPITALITY GROUP

Jyotsna Suri, chairperson and managing director, The Lalit Suri Hospitality Group, has been associated with the group since its inception in 1987. Ever since taking over as chairman and managing director in 2006, Suri has been the driving force of the group's operations across India. She spoke on a range of leadership issues. Excerpts from an interview:

How do you define a leader?

A leader must have a clear vision and the ability to lead his/her team towards achieving it. He/she should be able to overcome adversities and guide the organization through bad times.

What are the three most important traits of a leader?

A leader must be unbiased, patient and should possess people management skills.

As a leader of your group, how do you cultivate leaders?

By recognizing capabilities and delegating responsibilities accordingly.

Can a manager become a leader?

Leadership is inherent. However, it can be honed over a period of time. For a manager to become a leader, he/she should give equal opportunity to all; be patient and unbiased and recognize and nurture the strengths of team members as well as help overcome their weaknesses.

What is the role of a professional leader in a privately-promoted and a government-owned company?

Whether it is a privately-promoted or a government-owned company, the role of a leader remains the same—to have a clear vision and lead the team to achieve that vision.

Since September 2008, the world has seen a number of crises. What is the role of a leader in these times?

The role of a leader is to keep the morale of the employees high always, particularly during critical times and steer the organization out of the crisis.

What has been your biggest leadership challenge?

My biggest challenge was to give our brand a very strong and distinct identity. On 19 November 2008, I charted a brand change for the company. All luxury hotels now fly 'The Lalit' flag while the mid-segment hotels are branded as 'The Lalit Traveller', under The Lalit Suri Hospitality Group.

Leaders have to often carry the cross of other's wrongdoings and inefficiencies. What role can good leadership play to counterbalance this image?

A strong and successful leader should be able to take up challenges and guide his team irrespective of the wrongdoings and inefficiencies of others.

What is your one line leadership mantra?

Never give in.

Who are the leaders who have inspired you?

Mahatma Gandhi—a man who rose to become a force that single-handedly changed the history of India. Aung San Suu Kyi—a frail yet mentally strong woman who relentlessly fought for what she believed in.

Who is a leader in your industry whom you respect?

There is something to learn from each person I come across.

What is the biggest leadership lesson that you have learnt?

To stand for what you believe in, fearlessly. Also, leaders must give back to the society. As a hotelier, I believe in 'developing destinations', not just hotels. It is the people at the destinations that account for the success of the group's hotels and therefore our initiatives involve the local population, their handicrafts, culture, food, thereby giving them training and employment to boost the economic environment.

What is the best leadership decision that you have taken?

Rebranding the chain and initiating the 'developing destinations' concept.

What has been your worst leadership decision?

Out of thousands of decisions that one takes, there will be few which may not prove to be the best. However, I have no regrets.

ANUPAMA AIRY AND MAHUA VENKATESH

'Leaders make others lead': MOTILAL OSWAL,

CHAIRMAN, MOTILAL OSWAL FINANCIAL SERVICES

M otilal Oswal, chairman and managing director, Motilal Oswal Financial Services, has spent more than twenty-five years in the Indian financial market but says the stock market volatility still keeps him on his toes. Oswal spoke on a range of aspects on leadership. Excerpts from an interview:

How do you define a leader?

A leader has to think strategically and also needs to be very strong on execution. He/she should have capability to move from 50,000 feet to ground level. When it comes to execution, he needs to know what is happening at the ground level, and for strategy-making he needs to move to the highest possible level.

How do you spot a leader in your organization?

A person has to be very good on interpersonal skills and should be non-political. Ability to work as a team is also very important. He should be proactive in identifying in opportunities and solving problems and also be good in learning and reading. Presence of all these qualities makes it easy to identify a leader. A leader should be able to make his boss redundant. A leader should be able to do his boss's work.

How do you cultivate leaders in your organization?

We groom our people and we have a human resource department that runs a lot of programmes on leadership. If a person is ready to take responsibility, say if he/she is 60–70% ready, we give him the responsibility. You have to have confidence on your people. You need to take a bet that this guy will be able to perform. And, then we keep working on the process of mentoring and training.

Can you cite some examples of developing leaders in your organization?

We have many examples where people have risen to higher level from entry level. In our organization, we hire at lower level and keep on promoting them without hiring people at higher level from outside. Our internal auditor, who joined the organization 12–13 years ago, is now chief operating officer. Our head of research started his career in our company as an analyst, became senior analyst then covered some more sectors and then became head of research. Our CEO of institutional business joined as head of research then became head of sales and then became CEO. These examples send positive signals among other employees that if they perform they can also rise to the higher levels and strengthens the belief that the company believes in meritocracy.

What is your leadership style, are you a hands-on or hands-off leader?

I am a hands-on leader and I like to know what is going on. We have coffee with chairman, where I meet with officials at middle level. I like to meet employees through other ways to get the feel of how things are moving. For example, I don't have a reserve place in the canteen. I go and sit at any seat next to any employee for lunch. It's very important for me to know what is going at the ground level.

What is the biggest leadership challenge you have faced?

Volatility in the financial market is a major challenge. Sometimes we plan for x and get 2x but sometimes we plan for x but achieve only half of x. Attracting talent is also a major challenge, because being part of the financial services sector we have to compete globally.

As a leader do you regret any decision you have taken in the past?

I feel that some of my decisions relating to hiring people at higher level from outside proved wrong. A wrong hiring, at higher level, takes the company back couple of years.

Can managers become leaders or can leadership be learnt?

I think leadership traits can be acquired. There are very few born leaders. Leaders are created by circumstances, environment and organizations. A leader creates more leaders.

What is the role of a leader in a family-driven company?

In a family-driven company, a leader has two options. First is to groom a family member as a future leader and the second is to get a professional to lead the company. And both models work well. The only thing is that the leader has to be very clear whether he wants a family member or a professional from outside to lead the organization.

Who will lead your company—a person from family or a professional from outside?

It too early to decide about that, right now our entire focus is on growing the organization.

Which leaders have inspired you?

There are many business leaders who have inspired me. From India's business space I am inspired by Pawan Munjal (head of Hero MotoCorp), Rajiv Bajaj (MD, Bajaj Auto), Kumar Manglam Birla (chairman, Aditya Birla Group) and on international front I admire Sam Walton (founder, retailer Walmart), Steve Jobs (co-founder, chairman, and CEO of Apple) and Jack Welch (former chairman and CEO of General Electric).

Does leadership style varies from industry to industry or one leadership style fits all industries?

Softer skills such as grooming and mentoring, listening, communication and other interpersonal skills remain universal while technical skills vary from industry to industry. Also every leader would have strengths and weaknesses. For example, Steve Jobs was very strong in technical skills compared to softer skills while Jack Welch would be very strong in softer skills compared to technical knowledge.

What is your leadership mantra?

Whatever you do, do it with passion, half-hearted measures will not take you anywhere.

SACHIN KUMAR

'A good leader knows how to groom future ones': FERRUCCIO ROSSI,

CEO, FERRETTI GROUP

Ferruccio Rossi, chief executive officer of Ferretti Group, a luxury yatch maker, has worked as a consultant for KPMG Consulting for first three years of his career. In 1998, he became member of the investment banking team of ING Barings, and in 1999, he became the manager of investment banking team of JP Morgan Chase & Co., coordinating a lot of fusion and acquisition operations. Prior to his new appointment as Ferretti Group CEO, he was the America country manager of the group. Ferretti Group, headquartered at Forli, Italy, is a leader in the design, construction and marketing of luxury motor yachts. It has a popular portfolio of eight exclusive brands, each with its own distinctive features, including Ferretti Yachts, Pershing, Itama, Bertram, Riva, Mochi Craft, CRN and Ferretti Custom Line. In an interview, Rossi said that leadership is an incessant communication process whose success depends more on the perception of the employees about the ability of the leader, than on the leader himself. Edited excerpts:

What does leadership mean to you?

I believe the role of leaders is to inspire others. A leader must have the ability to inspire people to make them change direction. The key to success lies in the ability to promote leadership at all levels.

Who is your greatest inspiration?

Carlo Riva, the 'Pioneer of the Boating Industry', and Steve Jobs are two great sources of inspiration for me.

What is your leadership mantra? What is the most important trait of a leader?

An incessant communication process whose success depends more on the perception of the employees about the ability of the leader, than on the leader himself. Leadership involves building trusting relationships with your own working group to guide, lead the people to the achievement of organizational goals, creating opportunities for learning and growth, and bearing in mind that the ultimate goal of leadership is to groom new leaders.

How do you handle the bad economic scenario, especially when your performance is constantly watched?

It's important, in my opinion, to view this economic period as an opportunity to learn and improve our company in order to be ready for future chances. In any crisis, there are opportunities. The CEO's job is to spot them.

Is there a difference in leadership style when you manage business in India (a developing nation where luxury is still penetrating) and when you manage the Europe-based business?

India has price-conscious consumers. How do you compare the growth rate of the yacht business in India compared with the global growth and the growth five years ago?

For sure, India has recently started to approach the luxury market and only 0.6% of the total population belongs to the 'high' segment of the wealth pyramid. Thus, relatively to the leadership style, we have to consider a totally different penetrating strategy compared with other countries such as Europe. India can be considered a virgin territory for the nautical industry but, nowadays, a status symbol culture is developing also in this area and luxury brands in general are conquering a larger share market. Small marinas are developing along the west and the east coasts and yachting, sailing and charters have grown. On this basis, we think that the nautical industry may deliver good results over the next three to five years.

What is the best leadership decision you have taken so far?

My greatest satisfaction is to see in our company the success of young people which until their appointment were never considered by the 'common view' as candidates for the job.

And your worst decision as a leader?

I would not be a good leader if I had not taken any wrong decisions. The key thing is to learn from our mistakes (and also avoid to do too many).

Being a leader in world-class yacht brands, how do you keep a track on the not-so-wealthy consumers of India?

India is today one of the countries with the highest growth and has the best auspices for further growth over the coming years. We are experiencing great changes in both demographic and economic, and social situations.

Where does India stand for you as a focus market in the list of countries you look to expand business in? How do you plan to penetrate further into the country which is increasingly witnessing a luxury boom?

India does not look more to the generation who works abroad but to the growth of jobs in the country. The challenge is not about the past as a model, but on the simulation of the future. It is a country that is highly internationally reliable with a strong interest from Indian capital companies in foreign investments.

Any Indian leader, sports person or corporate leader you have taken notice of who has inspired you in some sense?

Surely, Mahatma Gandhi. Gandhi led India to independence employing non-violent civil disobedience and inspired movements for non-violence, civil rights and freedom across the world. A great leader!

It's important for a leader to walk the talk. What is your belief?

Respect comes from being able to do things. Actions speak louder than words and the results speak louder than actions. Confidence in the leader comes through honesty, trust and coherence between words and deeds, as well as the willingness to tackle difficult issues.

HIMANI CHANDNA GURTOO

'A leader must be a visionary': VENKATESH VALLURI,

CHAIRMAN AND PRESIDENT, INDIA, INGERSOLL RAND

Ingersoll Rand, a $14.0 billion (about Rs 77,000 crore) conglomerate has been in India for more than a hundred years and has been a pioneer of innovation in the industrial technology and climate solutions space. The company's India chairman and president, Venkatesh Valluri, spoke in an interview on various aspects of leadership. Excerpts:

How do you define a leader?

In my opinion, a leader is a visionary who is equipped with the skill set and knowledge to conceptualize and, further, to be able to pass on these traits to his team. He or she needs to be a thinker, with the ability to innovate, to take a risk and to conceive a solution or create a new market. Possessing the ability to engage people, collaborate and converge new technologies, products and services, a leader should be able to deliver solutions for the markets he or she is operating in.

What are the most important traits of a leader?

I think the 'ability to conceptualize' is one of the most important assets of a leader today. Another very important aspect of today's leader is his regard for engagement with the society. The fundamental measurement of delivering economic value does not change, but when coupled with social engagement, it signifies the social value being created. That is becoming the new definition of a leader in the organization.

As the leader of your company, how do you cultivate leaders?

Over the last two years we have been engaged in developing a world class leadership team that innovates, leads and builds world class solutions which effectively help advance the quality of life for emerging economies. We are infusing new talent as well as developing existing talent to create new opportunities not only for India but also allow our home grown technologies to be 'Reverse Globalized'.

Can leadership be learnt? In other words, how can a manager become a leader?

In today's world, a leader has to be able to address the needs of working and succeeding in a very ambiguous, uncertain and complex market place and yet be grounded with a value system that promotes authentic leadership. These, I believe are the new competencies required for this new world. The trick is to leverage their strengths while taking support in areas that may need development from their mentors and teams.

Do you think the role of business leaders has come under cloud —globally and domestically—of late?

I believe that an exemplary business leader is one who can foresee the changes that can occur in an environment domestically and globally and plan accordingly. A business leader is no longer an expert but has become the orchestrator for a different set of values and thought processes which were not present in the leadership lessons of the earlier decade. I guess they will always come under cloud when personal greed overtakes values and the sole purpose is to maximize individual gains and not be concerned about the sustainability of the business or the livelihood of thousands of employees who depend on it and the negative impact you make on the society or the environment.

Leaders have to often carry the cross of other's wrong doings and inefficiencies, the global banking sector today, for instance. What role can good leadership play to counterbalance this image?

There is a lesson, I learnt early in life. You do not spend more than fifteen minutes in rejoicing a win or repenting a loss. Move on. If you are the chosen one to lead, understand that you are not there to earn points by hiding behind someone else's inefficiencies of the past. The challenge for the leader is to steer the ship in a direction in which everyone believes in. The mark of a good leader therefore, is to learn to be collaborative but also be able to make the final call by taking in all contradicting inputs. Not everyone will always be on the bus. In such challenging times, leaders need to go back to the basics and ensure that they continue to display integrity, courage and authenticity. Motivating teams and discouraging despair and stagnation can help in continuous benchmarking.

What is your one line leadership mantra?

To me, the new leadership mantra is backed by 5 Cs—conceptualize, converge, collaborate, create and contribute. The core values of integrity and authenticity remain unchanged.

Who are the leaders that have inspired you?

I cannot name a single individual but I have taken lessons from a variety of people and how they operated in different environments. These have ranged from leaders in the armed forces, to corporate leaders, to people who have dedicated their lives to serve societies.

What is the biggest leadership lesson that you have learnt?

I strongly believe that one of the most important aspects of a leader is his regard for the society and his involvement in giving it back to the society. I think social responsibility is going to become a key deliverable of every company especially in emerging economies like India, and if a leader focuses on the customer, employee and society first, then shareholder value will automatically follow—but it is not going to be the other way around.

What is the best leadership decision you have taken?

Doing difficult roles others would not like to—the learning was tremendous.

What is the worst leadership decision you have taken?

I have not spent more than 15 minutes thinking about it—so I will not remember—but I will just say that I have made mistakes and I have learnt from them too!

GAURAV CHOUDHURY

'Involve employees in management': M. NARENDRA,

CHAIRMAN & MD, INDIAN OVERSEAS BANK

M Narendra, chairman and managing director, Indian Overseas Bank, has a unique way of functioning despite being in charge of a government-run bank. He believes that leaders need to be engaged with their employees while providing them the much- needed appreciation and encouragement. In an interview, Narendra said that promoting employees as a method of reward is a mantra he follows. Excerpts:

You have been leading a state-run bank. What according to you are the main challenges that this industry is facing at present?

Preparing people is a major challenge now. In the banking industry, especially public sector banks, recruitment has started taking place only in the past three years after a gap of about 10 years. This poses a challenge in the form of getting the newcomers ready to take over from the seniors who are retiring in large numbers. Despite many initiatives taken by the banks, image-building is another challenge. Coming out with a unique differentiator has become difficult. Leveraging of technology is a challenge. I feel that the capabilities of technology are yet to be fully tapped. Designing products enabled by technology will help not only in better customer acquisition but also reduce the cost of transactions.

As a leader do you find it difficult to steer the ship at a time when the economy is witnessing a sharp slowdown?

We are thankful to the government and the monetary authorities for carefully handling and taking remedial solution in the wake of the present economic slowdown. As such, we are ready to help the affected sectors. At the same time, our focus would continue to be on recovery and upgradation of NPAs (non-performing assets) and continuous monitoring of restructured accounts. I strongly believe that there would be a potential growth when banks help other segments when they are in dire need. In our long banking career, all of us have seen the ups and downs in the economy. It is important that prudent and cautious decisions and actions are taken during this period, so that when the recovery is complete, the banks are ready to lend more.

Has the going been tough?

Credit growth has been satisfactory. We are also focusing on recovery of non-performing assets. Fresh slippages are being monitored regularly.

What is your mantra as a leader?

'Energize, execute and excel' is the mantra I share with my colleagues. I enjoy my relationship with everyone. This helps in sharing the positive energy that each one of us possesses. I have total faith in God. This faith will give us more energy that what we believe we have. As we get that excess energy, our performance in day-to-day activities is enhanced. There will be superior quality in that performance that will ultimately result in excellence.

What is your leadership mantra?

I had always believed in involving employees in every aspect of management function. At IOB, where I have been the CMD since November 2010, I have ensured that the promotion processes happens at the time when they are due. The maximum number of promotions were given in the past three years. I also believe that there has to be conducive atmosphere in any organization to ensure its growth. A true leader has to ensure that this atmosphere is prevalent.

How do you plan to expand your reach over the next one year?

We have our own corporate medium and long-term plans covered under Vision and Mission Document 2013–2020. The strategies are well planned and the new slogan 'Touching Hearts, Spreading Smiles' created greater enthusiasm in the organization, inducing more vibrancy on the staff and our clientele. The bank continued its commitment towards financial inclusion in creating more depth in the rural market. During the year, the bank opened 273 branches across the country. Out of 273 branches opened during 2012–13, 188 branches are located in rural and semi-urban areas, of which 92 branches are located in unbanked rural centres.

There is an exodus of employees from public sector banks to the private sector. How do you address this as a leader?

I believe in giving what employees want—excellent recruitment practices, training opportunities, opportunities for promotion, recognition of performance and strong leadership.

MAHUA VENKATESH

'Leaders are those who empower others': SMINU JINDAL,

MD, JINDAL SAW

For Sminu Jindal, managing director, Jindal SAW, a part of the $10 billion OP Jindal Group, effective leadership requires a blend of both intellectual and emotional qualities. She spoke in an interview on a range of leadership issues. Excerpts:

How do you define a leader?

A leader is someone who can be admired, one who leads by example and not by words. I truly endorse the words of Bill Gates, 'As we look ahead into the next century, leaders will be those who empower others.' An effective leader requires a blend of both intellectual qualities—the ability to think analytically, strategically and creatively, and emotional ones, including self-awareness, empathy and humility. A leader should respond and not react to any given situation. Another important trait of a leader is to be resilient and approachable to his followers.

How do you cultivate leaders?

As a group, we believe in nurturing young minds to be innovative and add to the knowledge-pool of the organization.

How can a manager become a leader?

Leadership traits are inherent and can be further cultivated through resilience. Managers willing to accept new challenges and have conviction in their abilities can become leaders.

What is the role of a professional leader in a privately-promoted and a government-owned company?

The role of a leader is different in a privately-owned company and a government-owned company. Although in recent years, leadership styles have evolved minimizing such differences. The leadership is similar in terms of employee behaviour, social and environmental responsibility, risk-taking capacity, approach to decision-making and performance management.

What has been your biggest leadership challenge?

Being a woman, the biggest challenge for me was to break the glass ceiling in the steel, oil, and gas sector. Gender biases continue to play at different levels and that is one of the many disablers for a successful leadership. When the common perception was that women cannot perform in such male-dominated sectors and be good engineers, I busted both these myths.

Leaders have to often carry the cross of other's wrong-doings. What role can good leadership play to counterbalance this image?

Fortunately, I have not been through such a situation. But I believe that in these situations our commitment, experience and strong values come into play. We are vigilant in our enforcement towards corporate principles and are committed towards sustainable development and inclusive growth.

What is your one line leadership mantra?

I am greatly inspired by the thought shared by John C Maxwell, 'Leaders must be close enough to relate to others, but far enough ahead to motivate them.'

Who are the leaders who have inspired you?

My grandfather, late OP Jindal has truly inspired me as a leader. He always led by example. His generosity and humanity towards one and all had gone a long way in making our group a respected leader in the global steel industry.

What is the biggest leadership lesson you have learnt?

My capacity to grow determines my capacity to lead. This is the biggest leadership lesson I have learned during my tenure.

What is the best leadership decision you have taken?

I founded an initiative called 'Svayam' which advocates an enabling and accessible environment for all. Accessibility is an area for which many organizations are working.

What is the worst leadership decision you have taken?

There is no worst leadership decision taken as each and every resolution is well thought of.

GAURAV CHOUDHURY

'Encourage staff to break away from routines': HISAO TANAKA,

PRESIDENT & CEO, TOSHIBA CORP.

An avid reader and golfer, Hisao Tanaka has been the president and CEO of Toshiba Corporation since June 2013. Tanaka joined Toshiba in April 1973, and his diverse experience in procurement and manufacturing includes over 14 years of overseas assignments in the UK, the US and the Philippines. As a leader who encourages his employees to break away from routines, Tanaka believes it can be a powerful tool in generating breakthroughs and improvements. Excerpts from an interview:

What is leadership for you?

I think the essence of leadership is the ability to motivate every employee to be their very best. My mission is to provide the environment for that, lead them by defining a vision and direction that everyone can share. The challenge for me is to understand how to concentrate the capabilities of 2,00,000 employees around the world, and channelize them into making Toshiba a premium company that takes the best practices from different business units.

Who is your greatest inspiration?

All the people I have encountered had an effect on me, including my ex bosses, colleagues, friends, family and parents.

What is your leadership mantra?

Communication, openness and fairness in discussion is the essence of leading an organization. The most important and strongest factor in achieving a target is making sure that everybody in the organization shares the same understandings; that there is a harmony of intention that encourages each individual to carry out his or her mission. And that can only be secured through communication. There is need to discuss issues to get different perspectives and from that arrive at the best answer.

How does a leader manage the bad economic scenario, especially when your performance is being constantly watched?

My management policy is based on a vision of growth through creativity and innovation. This means pursuing growth that is not overly dependent on the growth of the market but generated by the company's own creative powers. I also challenge our employees to start thinking from scratch, from zero, and to reject current ways of doing business or working. It is very difficult to break away from routines you are used to, but doing so can be a powerful tool to generate breakthroughs.

How a leader turns cultural barriers to his/her advantage?

I have worked in the US, Europe, and the Philippines, and my experience has taught me that every region has a different business culture. Management style in the US is top-down and values fast decision-making, which is different from the Japanese or Asian style. Experience is the best teacher.

What is the best leadership decision you have taken so far?

It is difficult to point to one particular decision and say, 'That's it!' My choice of management style and my experience of working in different fields make me think of things from scratch and begin by building up to a new grand design. For me, this approach leads to good decision-making.

And your worst decision?

I try not to make them. Being a leader in electronics, how do you track the innovations across the globe?
Toshiba's research and development expenditure is about 300 billion yen a year, around 5% of sales. In addition to our R&D centres in Japan, we have research operations in the US, Europe, China, and software development bases in India and Vietnam. This global scope is an important factor in our competitiveness.

Is India an important market for you?

In terms of sales, Japan, the US and China are our three big countries today. However, in recent years, India has ranked among the most attractive investment destinations for many Japanese firms, because of the country's high economic growth and robust consumption. Above all, India has good reputation in tertiary education, and that's one reason why we established a software development base in Bangalore, and then set up a joint venture with JSW group in manufacturing steam turbines and generators in Chennai.

What are your investment plans in India for the next three years?

We will invest over 3,000 crore in India over the next five years and create employment for over 5,000 people.

Any Indian leader who inspires you?

Sachin Tendulkar immediately comes to my mind. I admire his achievements and constant quest for the highest level of performance, always seeking to be better.

It is important for a leader to speak through actions. What is your take on it?

I absolutely agree. I believe it is important to actually go to the place, see what needs to be done and only then speak, to communicate solutions. I always try to hold discussion sessions with the people working there when I visit subsidiaries or branch offices. That is my approach. Look and act, then speak.

HIMANI CHANDNA GURTOO

'Leaders have to create their own path': MILIND BARVE,

MANAGING DIRECTOR, HDFC ASSET MANAGEMENT COMPANY

Milind Barve, managing director of HDFC Asset Management Company, which manages HDFC's mutual funds, has spent about thirty years with the company. Prior to his current assignment, he headed HDFC's treasury operations and then, its retail deposit products. In this interview, he discusses his leadership mantra. Excerpts:

How do you define a leader?

A leader is one who builds a high quality team by creating an environment where talent is nurtured and retained. He has to give his team a clear strategic direction and take responsibility for decisions taken. This is all the more relevant for the financial services industry, which is very people-dependent.

How do you nurture young executives into leaders?

The quality of talent we hire is exceptionally good. Our job is to give them the right environment to grow. For that, we have to ensure a professional and impartial environment and give them the right degree of empowerment. Most people, I've noticed enjoy work. The early stages of one's career should be devoted to learning. You cannot become a leader if your knowledge base is hollow. Also, looking good and talking well are not enough to make you a leader. You need integrity and team spirit to be a leader.

Can you learn leadership?

No. You can't learn leadership. You must have qualities that can be nurtured. A mentor can give you exposure. But leadership is not something everyone can take on. You have to create your own path. Peer pressure, how you react to situations and crises and the fire in your belly show you the way. The last few years have seen many ups and downs. The markets have see-sawed; the economy has teetered on the brink.

How did you, as a leader, keep up the morale of your team?

It's darkest before dawn. Equity as an asset class is good when the markets are down. I had to encourage my team to swim against the tide. People seldom say they have no money to invest. They are always looking for investment avenues. But it isn't easy to change peoples' asset allocations.

If a client chose debt, I would encourage my team to give him the best options available. I kept my teams motivated by engaging more with them and pushed them to diagnose and identify the pulse of the client in order to serve him better.

What is the biggest leadership challenge you've faced?

It has to be the 2008 crisis. At times like that it becomes our responsibility to take leadership of the industry—meeting people from Sebi, RBI, the finance ministry and other decision makers to help tide over bad times. There was a drop in confidence in the financial markets. Bank FDs became popular. It was a really testing time.

You have moved from heading HDFC's treasury operations to heading its retail deposit products to now heading the MF operations. As a leader, how did you make the transition?

You can never be a leader if you don't understand your product. You have to learn if you don't know. As head of treasury at HDFC, I was managing a corpus of Rs 7,000–8,000 crore. Unless I built a corpus of at least Rs 8,000 crore at HDFC AMC, my new job would seem like a demotion. Since it was a new company, I had to get people from diverse backgrounds, build a new team and create a culture closest to HDFC—open, informal, flat with high standards of ethics and integrity.

What is your leadership mantra?

Delegate and supervise.

What is the biggest leadership lesson you have learnt?

As your company grows large, you cannot be a hands-on manager. Earlier, I would check reconciliation statements, meet customers, etc., but learnt to play the real role of a leader—decide strategy, supervise implementation, empower teams and give myself the time to look at the big picture. Scale is important but profitability is the ultimate barometer to judge success.

What is the best leadership decision you have taken?

Acquiring Zurich AMC in 2003. Zurich offered a great strategic fit. It was known for equity, we were known for debt.

What is the worst leadership decision you have taken?

We have still not built a meaningfully large international business.

Who are your role models?

HDFC Ltd chairman Deepak Parekh. He has proved that you can be simple, upright, honest and yet successful.

ARNAB MITRA

'Leaders must create transparent cultures': MILIND SHAH,

VICE-PRESIDENT, MEDTRONIC

Milind Shah, vice-president for South Asia at Medtronic, is responsible for driving the the $16.6 billion US-based medical devices giant's expansion and growth in the region, in addition to running the company's entire operations for South Asia. He had joined as the managing director of India Medtronic in October 2004. He spoke on a range of issues on leadership in an interview. Excerpts:

What is leadership for you?

To me leadership is about creating and articulating a shared vision, gaining alignment and enabling the organization to progress towards the goal. Leadership means enabling the organization with the right resources and structure, getting the right people on board and establishing and achieving milestones through trust and delegation. Leadership is also about establishing the right culture of transparency, accountability, speed and smart risk taking.

How do leaders manage the bad economic scenario?

Every business goes through cycles, and it is imperative that the leader understands this. This enables her not to get carried away in good times while remaining calm and focus on learning during the difficult periods. Downturns require the leader to demonstrate edge to take tough calls and communicate these clearly to all the stakeholders. Finally, being better prepared than other players creates exciting new opportunities in challenging circumstances.

Is there a difference in leadership style when you manage business in India (a developing nation) and when you manage business in developed markets?

In my opinion, the basic leadership tenets remains the same, regardless of the market. However, the opportunities and challenges may vary in design and content as businesses are typically at different stages in the business cycle in emerging markets as compared to the developed markets. Business in emerging markets is very dynamic, while in developed markets it might be a little more predictable or the changes may not be as sudden or forceful. To manage this, the emerging markets leader has to have strong peripheral vision, be entrepreneurial and have the ability to drive change. Also, the emerging world has many more market segments. This leads to a lot of innovation, both in technology and business models and often these innovations find their way into the developed world. Ignoring these could, therefore, not only impact the business in emerging markets but also the developed world.

What is the best leadership decision that you have taken so far?

One of our good decisions has been to invest in Healthy Heart for All, a business model innovation in India. This business model has helped develop a holistic solution for multiple barriers that a patient faces in the care pathway.

And your worst decision as a leader?

Once I hired a person without due diligence on his credentials—and realized that he was not the right person for that position at that particular phase of the business cycle. As a result the business suffered, and the individual too. Ultimately, of course we parted ways. But it was a lesson learnt.

Being a leader in medical devices technology, how do you keep a track of the innovations across the globe?

Medtronic's leadership in innovation is itself a part of the answer. We invest significant resources in cranking our innovation engine and much of our work is cutting edge. We have a very open and transparent culture that not only allows for, but also makes it essential to keep track of innovations and technological breakthroughs.

Any Indian leader who inspired you in some sense?

'The Wall', I find Rahul Dravid a very inspiring leader, one of the best examples of a leader with great focus and grit, and yet so unassuming. His ability to deal with ups and downs, and continuous adaptability are a few qualities that I greatly admire and aspire to imbibe.

It's important for a leader to watch his words speak through actions. What is your belief?

Walking the talk is ultimately something you do at a personal level, and it is one of the most important traits of a good leader. It is very important to lead by example, not only to inspire your team but also to show that you mean what you say and that you say what you mean. It's proof of your credibility, intent and reliability. I do believe, one needs to be carefully authentic, humane and not make impassioned speeches that lack compassion.

GAURAV CHOUDHURY

'Learning comes from your customers': USHA ANANTHASUBRAMANIAN,

CHAIRPERSON AND MD, BHARATIYA
MAHILA BANK

Usha Ananthasubramanian has taken over as chairperson and managing director, Bharatiya Mahila Bank (BMB), believes it is critical to empower women in the country. The bank has 150–160 employees at present but plans to add 50 more jobs. Women account for 70% of the workforce. Ananthasubramanian says that it is not easy for a woman at the workplace because she is constantly being watched. Excerpts from an interview:

You have taken over as chief of BMB that has been in focus for its unique proposition. How do you hope to incentivize your staff especially with limited scope to give rewards in monetary terms like the private sector?

Clearly, the opportunities are tremendous in the public sector banking space and especially in BMB since it is a new bank and has a clear focus. I agree money is important but that is not the only thing. Here you get an exposure that is simply unique. You get to work with two kinds of India, one is the underserved and underpenetrated, and at the same time you are serving the opulent and forward looking population. So the career opportunity, exposure and experience that you gain are very enriching and you cannot match that.

According to you what are the main challenges that the industry faces?

I can speak about public sector banks. I would say that one of the biggest challenges is talent crunch and something needs to be done to address the issue. The weakest segment is human resource. Once you acquire talent, you need to retain talent and in today's environment, you need to find ways to retain talent. When we started work—say 25–30 years ago—there were limited opportunities but today there are multiple options and opportunities. So the most important things that banks need to focus on are acquire, nurture and retain talent.

In this scenario, how do you motivate your staff and how did you draw talent to BMB?

One needs to find ways to motivate people even if you cannot give remunerations, which match the private sector. For example, here, we offered a higher designation to everybody, who came forth. Basically we gave them a promotion—one notch higher than his or her earlier designation. Besides, since BMB has a clear mandate, there is also a lot of curiosity around it. People want to join the bank. They want to make it a success and they want to give it a try.

As a leader, how do you think talent can be retained?

Most importantly, talent must be recognized and that is very important and the senior management plays a key role. So first, you recognize and then look at motivating them through fast-track promotions. Out-of-the-box ideas are essential to nurture and retain talent. A leader also needs to engage with people on a regular basis.

Several new banks are expected to come in by the end of the year. Do you see any threats?

New banks will come in, which is very good. But yes, there could be migration and we must understand that and act from now on. We need to look at human resource very critically and treat our people as our assets.

What is your leadership mantra?

I believe in three things—credibility, visibility and accessibility. You need credibility for acceptance and for that you need to focus on visibility. And for these, you need to be with your team. Your team must have full faith in you. You need to be accessible to both your customers and staff. You need to understand their requirements and you also need to know what is happening at the ground level. You cannot lose touch with either your customers or staff. You cannot be living in an ivory tower; all the learning will come from your customers.

Who are your role models?

Former Bank of Baroda Chairman and Managing Director Anil Khandelwal is one person I look up to. I have learnt a lot from him. He has helped me understand how the top level operates. Besides, I take inspiration from JRD Tata. The biggest learning of my life is that you need to be a fine human being at the end of the day.

What problems do women face in the workforce?

Honestly, as a woman, it is not easy as you will be watched continuously and there is tremendous pressure on you not to make mistakes. As a woman, you have to be known to be hard-working and intelligent. For a man, his career determines his success, while for a woman, it is her career, home and various other paradigms.

As a woman leader, what would you like to share?

When a woman is at the top, she becomes a loner. Men do a lot of networking, women generally do not do that. There is also another face that a woman has—where she is in search of some creativity for herself that is beyond work—that creative space gives her immense satisfaction. It could be anything—cooking, singing and story-writing. When women reach the top, they need a lot of emotional support from the office and home.

MAHUA VENKATESH

'A leader must not beat around the bush': ERICK HASKELL,

MANAGING DIRECTOR, ADIDAS INDIA

Erick Haskell, MD, Adidas India, says that a leader should have the ability to take hard decisions and should regard integrity of people as a non-negotiable principle. In an interview, he said that leadership is followership. Excerpts:

How difficult was it to lead the company given the controversies surrounding Adidas and Reebok in India?

I won't lie. It was difficult time for the company in general. I think the biggest challenge when I came in was to take all the stakeholders—employees, suppliers and franchises through a rough ride. The challenge for me as a leader was to pick all these people up and get them motivated and say look, this is a fantastic brand and has an amazing history in this country, it has a deep tie with Indian consumers, so let us put this behind us and move forward. As a leader, the most difficult thing was to get back people in the mindset to look forward and rebuild. That took a few months for me to tell people to really focus on the future rather than focusing on something that we have been through.

How do you define leadership?

I would define leadership as followership. I really think what defines a good leader is one who takes hard decisions. It may not necessarily be popular at times or it may be a decision people would not agree with. But if you are a good leader and you know that something is fundamentally correct and it's the right path, you need to follow that.

How often have you taken unpopular decisions, and if you can specify some of those?

Rather than unpopular, I would say difficult decisions and it is frequent because we are in a rapidly-changing industry in a highly competitive environment. For example, our business (in India) runs largely through a franchise model. It's a difficult model to run a business on but it's the best model as well to present a brand in a country. We took a decision, during the crisis, to stick to it and continue to back it that rather than going through the distributor model. In retrospect, it was a good decision.

How difficult is the transition from a manager to a CEO?

It's difficult. It comes down to the question: are leaders born or made? I think you can learn leadership and I would go back to the statement I made about taking hard decisions. I don't think someone can be a good professional manager without the ability to take hard decisions.

Which is the worst leadership decision you have taken?

The hardest decision you have to take is coming face to face with someone who is not performing. And early during my executive career I found it a difficult thing to do and I regret when you don't take hard decisions on people.

How important communication is in such a situation, and generally, for a leader?

Communication in general, and performance issues, is absolutely critical. I found out is that when you generally confront someone with the fact that they are not performing up to the mark, you should let them know where they stand. If you want to put a very ambitious plan, then every person on board has to live up to that plan on a daily basis to accomplish it.

What are your views on succession planning, especially for corporations like yours?

It's critical. In fact, it was probably within my first six months when I was here I took all my executive team off sites, we locked ourselves in one room for a full day and we completed our entire succession planning exercise.

Who are the leaders who have inspired you?

I am inspired by people who are extremely principled and everything they do ties back to that principle. So from American history, Dr Martin Luther King is a person whom I really got inspired by because he had extraordinary principles and he never wavered from those core principles. And there is an interesting Indian connection there because most of his philosophy is inspired by Mahatma Gandhi. So I have been drawn to such leaders who stand by their principles and fight for it.

Which are the principles that are non-negotiable for you?

Integrity and honesty are the most important and absolutely non-negotiable principles for me. Particularly in a work environment, the direct transparent way of working; I don't like beating around the bush. I like honest, direct, integrity-based people.

What is your leadership mantra?

'Leading by example'. It's extremely powerful and I show my team everyday what is expected out of me in terms of deliverables.

GAURAV CHOUDHURY

'A leader must stay calm during challenges': PRAMOD CHAUDHARI,

EXECUTIVE CHAIRMAN, PRAJ INDUSTRIES

Praj Industries, provider of ethanol solutions, came into spotlight a few years ago when ethanol started gaining global importance as an alternative renewable source of fuel. But things took a turn for the worse as the food-versus-fuels debate slowed the bio-fuels industry. As executive chairman of Praj Industries, Pramod Chaudhari was faced with the challenge of reducing his company's dependence on the ethanol business and to diversify into newer areas such as projects to treat industrial waste water and providing water solutions to pharma, cosmetics and the food & beverage industry. Chaudhari said in an interview that encouraging people to accept the change has been his biggest leadership challenge. Excerpts:

How do you define a leader?

A leader is a visionary. He is someone who guides his team and provides the big picture and the guiding principles. He is the one who sees beyond the present time and sets the goal for the future. A true leader will always be optimistic and seek learning from his failures, but will never look back.

What are the three most important traits of a leader?

A leader is a change agent, who takes bold but calculated risks and converts them into successful ventures. They challenge the existing paradigms and think out of the box. Secondly, networking and maintaining a good relationship with all stakeholders is another essential quality of a leader. Trusting and sharing his vision with his people and delegating work effectively are also equally important to take his ideas to the next level. Third and one of the most critical qualities is to act calm when he is faced with challenges. Haste and anger might lead to a wrong decision and that is why leaders need to remain strong while dealing with crisis.

As a leader of your company, how do you cultivate leaders?

We believe in providing equal opportunity to people in expressing their views and we have methods in place to identify leadership qualities and skills in ordinary people. We identify potential leaders based on formal and informal interactions and then we have in place a full-fledged leadership development program to turn them into leaders of tomorrow. The tough job, however, is in identifying the true potential leaders.

Can leadership be learnt? In other words, how can a manager become a leader?

You need not be a born leader. It is a matter of realization and conditioning. I would encourage an ordinary worker with extraordinary shopfloor skills to understand the nuances of leadership and how he/she can combine his/her skills with management and people skills to become a good leader. We encourage our managers to take initiatives, give them opportunities to demonstrate and prove their skills and ensure classroom and on-the-grounds trainings to turn them into potential leaders. The world has been hit by series of financial crisis in recent years. The ethanol industry, where your expertise lies, has also seen its ups and downs.

What is the role of the leader in such times?

Ups and downs are part of any business. We have used the period of crisis to move from being a pure engineering company to an engineering solutions company for ethanol business, driven by innovation and integration capabilities and acquisitions. As a leader, I should be able to see opportunity in adversity and take this opportunity to move up the value chain and emerge stronger.

What has been the biggest leadership challenge that you have faced?

The biggest leadership challenge that I have faced is encouraging people to accept change. In any business, changes are inevitable if you have to be in sync with the times. Many people resist change, which makes it challenging for a leader to make them focus on their goals. Leaders have to often carry the cross of other's wrongdoings and inefficiencies.

What role can good leadership play to counterbalance this image?

A leader is someone who also has to take responsibility of other people's actions by virtue of his/her position. It could be an error of judgment or lack of proper communication that could have led to the failure. A leader must be able to identify the root cause of the problem and work towards remedying it. However, a leader should be able to take tough decisions if it comes to that.

What is your one line leadership mantra?

Leadership is not about controlling, it is about taking people along with you.

NACHIKET KELKAR

'A leader must have the ability to envision the future': RAJIV BAJAJ,

VICE-CHAIRMAN & MANAGING DIRECTOR, BAJAJ CAPITAL

Rajiv Bajaj, vice-chairman and managing director, Bajaj Capital, took over the leadership role in 1990 from his father K.K. Bajaj, who is the founder and chairman of the investment services company. The company, which was formed fifty years ago on 19 February, was the first to get into the personal finance and investment space at a time when the segment was primarily dominated by individual players. In an interview, the junior Bajaj said that convincing his boss, who is also his father, is one of the toughest things. He says people are influenced when you walk the talk and be modest. Excerpts:

With concerns, such as regulatory changes and a slowdown, among other concerns, which may be impacting your business, how do you overcome these?

A slowdown means that you have to think and work harder to get the same results—it takes a toll on the mind and one needs to develop emotional resilience to handle this period. In India, we have rule-based regulations, and not principle-based. Hence, it sometimes gets stifling to execute your vision in true earnest. In this era of social and political activism, I spend 10% of my time trying to work as a volunteer, working on solutions for industry issues. It may not give immediate results, but it gives solace.

How do you motivate your employees?

I stay connected. From my experience, I feel that people get disoriented when you become aloof. On the other hand, they love it when you listen to them with undivided attention. So, you need to engage with them, make them feel valuable.

As a family-run business, is making a decision easy?

It is not easy to take decisions in a family-run business contrary to popular belief. There could be others too with differing opinions and often it takes a longer time. Everyone has his/her own perspective, and influencing people is the toughest job that a leader has to perform. My experience is that people are influenced when you walk the talk. You also have to be persistent and keep repeating your expectations like a broken record.

What has been the biggest leadership challenge you have faced?

The biggest challenge for me in this context has been to make my point of view understood to my boss who is also my father. It is very difficult to have your own father as a boss, since professionalism and emotions get mixed up most of the time. But he is my best friend too and we spend a lot of time informally also—talking things out and coming to an acceptable solution. Most things are sorted out, but I haven't been able to convince him to accept my point of view on making Saturdays a holiday for the organization (Saturday is a working day for us at present).

What is your leadership mantra?

Be modest. I truly believe that there is a lot more to be achieved and I am not even close to where I want to reach and I make sure everyone in your company feels the same way.

Who are the leaders whom you look up to?

No one, really. I pick up good points from everyone, even from my watchman. Pieces of wisdom are there all around you, you just need to keep an eye out for it. I learn everyday and from everybody. I try and learn ten new things every day.

What are the challenges that you face at work, and how do you solve them as a leader?

There are no challenges really. It is all in the mind. I try to be positive most of the time, and keep telling myself that this storm too shall pass. The worst thing is to freeze in a crisis.

What is the most important trait a leader must have?

The ability to envision the future and communicate it down to the very last person in the organization.

What does leadership mean to you?

Being a servant. You can't lead till you learn to serve—your clients, your team.

MAHUA VENKATESH

'A good leader needs to listen to customers': FERRUCCIO FERRAGAMO,

CHAIRMAN, SALVATORE FERRAGAMO ITALIA SPA

Chairman of luxury brand Salvatore Ferragamo Italia Spa, Ferruccio Ferragamo, believes that a true leader not only knows the market, but also listens to customers and their needs. Ferragamo discusses a range of leadership issues in an interview. Excerpts:

What are the essential qualities of a true leader?

I believe a true leader not only knows his/her market, but also listens to its customers and understands their needs, staying a step ahead of the times in supply and markets.

To be a leader, what are the essential things required in an emerging market like India?

Know your customers, their tastes and their needs but, above all, offer products known for their excellent quality.

About ten years ago, many luxury brands including yours had seen India as a leader among the emerging markets. How do you see India now?

India is a large country with immense potential, which will be able to take shape when its infrastructure begins to consolidate.

Ever since you assumed charge as the chairman of Salvatore Ferragamo, what are the things that you introduced in the brand strategies that made a difference to your business?

As far as Ferragamo's strategy is concerned, one of our greatest strengths is that we have focused on tradition and continuity, adjusting and developing a new cultural approach over time, while also focusing on gaining a widespread worldwide presence across all distribution channels, and retail in particular, to fully meet our global clientele's expectations. The decision to embrace traditional Italian craftsmanship underscores the fundamental importance that fine craftsmanship holds for the company still today. Indeed, the craftsman's role is not merely that of an expert worker, but it is his ability to do things with excellence, or, as one would say in Italian, a regola d'arte, with an eye to detail. It is work that requires time, passion and constancy, but that creates one-of-a-kind pieces. The craftsman is an expert, and Salvatore Ferragamo's success lies in the dedication and creativity of all the people who make it up.

How do you compare the Indian market with that of other emerging markets?

I would say that every emerging market has its own historic, social and cultural characteristics, making them difficult to compare.

As a leader what is the best decision that you have taken?

We have taken many important decisions over the years. To name just one, the listing on the Milan stock exchange was a step in which our entire family takes great pride. The initial public offer (IPO) was a crucial strategic decision that has given us significant international visibility and is making it possible for us to pursue the growth strategy that we have outlined over the years.

Any bad decision that you regret?

Nothing comes to mind, perhaps because it is easier to remember positive decisions than it is to recall the negative ones.

What are your expansion plans for India?

We are attentively watching the country and its development. For the time being, we do not have any specific plans, but it is a market that we are carefully monitoring.

Do you have plans for using any raw material from India for your products? Have you ever used any from India in the past?

Our company's products are 'Made in Italy' and that is our focus, although India clearly boasts myriad high-quality raw materials that could be used to make excellent products. Salvatore Ferragamo is considered the leader in the leather luxury goods segment.

What do you attribute this success to?

Salvatore Ferragamo embodies a combination of consolidated, expert craftsmanship and the creative tradition, typical of 'Made in Italy' products. These forms of excellence bolster the brand and have, over the years, developed in line with its origins, while enabling us to grow globally. Quality, contemporary elegance and innovation are the hallmarks of each and every Ferragamo product and I believe that, along with our tradition of fine craftsmanship, they are what has led to the brand's widely recognized value and authenticity.

VINOD NAIR

'Leaders must take the best from everyone': NIMESH SHAH,

CEO & MD , ICICI PRUDENTIAL AMC

Nimesh Shah, a chartered accountant by profession, took over as the managing director and chief executive officer of ICICI Prudential AMC in July 2007. Since then he has steered the company and helped thousands in becoming richer. Before this, Shah was senior general manager at ICICI Bank where he was involved with project finance, corporate banking and international banking. Shah says saving is not good enough, converting the savings into investment is more important. Shah spoke in an interview on several leadership aspects. Excerpts:

What drives you as a leader?

Having a significantly positive effect on investors' wealth and facilitating best investment practices is a driving force for me. Managing other people's money is a huge responsibility; it is our resolve to give good risk-adjusted returns to investors. We have done so for several years in the past and want to be recognized for this. In an inflationary economy, saving is not good enough; converting the savings into investment is more important. This is where we come in: to guide the common man to convert his savings into investments.

What is your mantra?

Keep the customer's interest at the helm of the organization's objective; then, everything else falls into place. This mantra has helped us to transform our fund house to an entirely investor-centric company offering investors not only a product suite that caters to their every possible need, but also creating significant value for them by managing their money well.

How do you build loyalty among your team members?

Aligning individual aspirations of performing employees and nurturing them through lateral and horizontal growth opportunities has helped us to build loyalty among team members. A culture that is built on mutual trust and respect for all stakeholders helps this.

Any decision you felt may have gone wrong?

Not every decision made can go right. The fear of a decision going wrong shouldn't stop one from taking decisions with conviction. For instance, in July 2012 we launched a fund that invests in the US equities and the fund has given excellent returns to investors since inception. The regret is that we could not get more investors into the scheme at the time of the launch so that they could also benefit. But the fear of mis-selling keeps us away from being pushy in promoting schemes.

What is the best decision that you have taken?

On commencement of my association with ICICI Prudential, my mandate was not a grassroot incubation project, but to shape and manage its evolution within the emerging and challenging environment. The key focus area of improvement was to evolve the organization from a sales-led one to a holistically investor-centric one. While we were aware of the challenges of this task, we knew it was achievable. Over the past few years, we have consciously worked at these aspects with the sole objective of providing our investors a good investment experience. The recent recognition of our AMC (asset management company) through various awards is a reaffirmation and an acknowledgement of our efforts.

Who are your role models?

It is hard to label one particular role model in my life. Emulation is the best form of learning. I firmly believe that there is something to learn from every individual and, being a keen observer of people and practices, I emulate the best from everyone around me.

Compared to the other developed economies, how do you see the mutual funds industry developing in India?

Globally, a significant portion of growth in the mutual fund industry has come from household retirement savings. The mutual fund industry in the western world took off by initiating a strong pull strategy—attracting money from pension funds as well as offering tax advantage to mutual fund investors. In the Indian scenario, the mutual fund industry is at a nascent stage and while foreign pension funds are investing in India, we are yet to see key reforms on the domestic pension side. The other significant enabler for capital formation and development of this industry can be in the form of growth of 'equity culture' by virtue of incentivizing equity investing for retail investors.

MAHUA VENKATESH

'Leaders must inspire others to trust them': DIANA NELSON,

CHAIRPERSON, CARLSON

Diana Nelson's election to chairman of Carlson, a privately held, global hospitality and travel company that runs hotels under Radisson, Country Inns & Suites By Carlson, Park Inn and Park Plaza brands, marks the passing of leadership to the third generation of the Carlson family. Nelson is only the third person to serve in this capacity in the company's 75-year-old history. She spoke in an interview on a range of leadership issues. Excerpts:

How do you define a leader?

Leaders start with a vision. Having vision requires clarity of purpose and direction. Leaders need to have the ability to communicate and motivate people to work towards the vision. It is important that they can inspire others to trust and support them.

What are the three most important traits of a leader?

I believe that the most important trait of a leader is authenticity and self knowledge. You need to know your values and belief system. This self-knowledge is a compass for navigating complex situations. Secondly, in order to lead, one should have clarity of vision and the ability to communicate it. The obstacle to good communications is our lens on the world. Each of us is informed differently and our view of the world is seen through our own lens and that may be opaque to someone else. A great example of seeing through a different lens can be found in a family with different generations. The third trait is curiosity. Leadership is about change. The ability to respond to change is particularly critical for business leaders today as the pace of innovation is very rapid.

What is the role of a professional leader in a family business?

Previously, my grandfather, uncle and mother held the position of CEO. When my mother was ready to retire, we recognized it would be challenging to maintain a policy of family leadership in the top operating role. We debated at length and agreed that it was most important that the company be well managed and continue to grow profitably to benefit its shareholders. Having a symbolic leader would be in conflict with this vision. So, in our 70th year of business we appointed our first non-family CEO, Hubert Joly, who had been leading Carlson Wagonlit Travel. Carlson made a successful transition to non family management and we now have our second non-family CEO, Trudy Rautio.

How do you deal with challenges in a family-run business?

Our family shareholders have been proactively learning best practices for sustaining a closely-held business over generations. We wrestle out issues together to arrive at a solution that is in line with our vision to benefit the business and shareholders. It is sometimes inevitable to have conflicts as board members and family members are from different backgrounds, various parts of the country and age groups.

What is the biggest worry in this process of leadership model?

The thing that I worry most about is transition. My generation, which is the third generation, has a clear view of the founder, my grandfather, who had full control of the business. We know his values. Of the seven members of the third generation, five are actively involved in corporate governance. The next generation will be larger and more distanced from the company's origins. Their challenges will include selecting a smaller subset of family members to represent others in governance and balancing collective versus individual achievement.

What is the worst leadership decision you have taken?

It is hard to pinpoint a worst decision as judgment is usually made in the present context. But I am concerned about how we reshape our investment portfolio. I am particularly aware that any time we divest of a line of business it is a momentous decision. Five years later, we can't go back and change the decision.

Who are the leaders that have inspired you?

There are leaders in many sectors who are inspirational. One of them is Drew Gilpin Faust. She is a historian and became president of Harvard University when Harvard was going through a tough time during the economic downturn. I also take inspiration from Sheryl Sandberg, chief operating officer of Facebook. She has been an important voice for women.

GAURAV CHOUDHURY

'A leader has to work harder than others': NILESH SHAH,

MD & CEO, AXIS CAPITAL

Nilesh Shah, who took over as managing director and CEO of Axis Capital, wholly-owned subsidary of Axis Bank, last October, has created a reputation for being very people-centric in his approach to business. Here, he talks about what it takes to be a leader. Excerpts:

How do you define a leader?

A leader is someone who sets goals, mostly stretched ones, and mobilizes his team to achieve those seemingly difficult goals with relative ease.

How do you nurture young executives into leaders?

I like to throw them into the deep end. If they are smart, they'll learn how to swim… I don't give them a life jacket but give them tasks to motivate them. My job as a leader is to guide them but they have to learn to walk or swim on their own. And my experience is that given the right guidance, most people will learn to swim to the other end.

Can you teach people leadership? How?

Yes. I have seen many young men and women, who everyone had written off, shine and become top performers once they were given proper guidance. You have to lead people, motivate them to deliver, show that you have confidence and faith in their ability. People can do a lot and surprise you with superlative performance if you do that. The last few years have seen many ups and down. The markets have see-sawed, the economy has teetered on the brink.

How did you, as a leader, keep up the morale of your team?

We used to call the 1857 uprising against the British a mutiny. But now, we call it the First Battle of Independence. In India, we like to paint a picture of ourselves that's worse than reality. Many investors abroad have told me: 'If you stop denigrating yourself, you will be better off.' If you keep the bigger picture in mind, stick to fundamentals, you will see long-term gains, not the short-term pain. That's what I told my team when the times became tough. I told them to see how they could solve our clients' problems and create value… You have to work harder during difficult times. If you do that, the rest will fall into place.

What is the biggest leadership challenge you've faced?

When I first became the leader of my team, I realized that I shouldn't try to fill someone else's shoes because everyone has a different style and people's expectations from new leaders are often unrealistic. Then, over time, teams get used to a particular comfort zone. Unless you shake them up, you can't take it to the next orbit. Fortunately, I had never thought of myself as a second in command, so the transition to a leadership position didn't matter much. It only meant added responsibility.

What's your leadership mantra?

Be critical but fair. Then, a leader has to work harder than anyone else. There is no substitute to hard work. I try to lead from the front. It's very important to earn the respect of your team.

What is the biggest leadership lesson that you have learnt?

Just keep your focus. I have to deliver only on one thing… A leader has to remove hurdles—especially the seemingly insurmountable ones that my team faces from time to time. If I can do that, I'm fulfilling my role as a leader.

What is the best leadership decision you have taken?

Over the last 20 years, most people I have worked with have become a part of my extended family. What began as an official relationship, became a bonding for life—where there is mutual respect, trust and admiration. It feels good to have been able to foster such an environment at work. When I look back, I feel that everything that went into creating such lasting relationships were good decisions.

What is the worst leadership decision you have taken?

That I had to let go of people during tough times. I feel that process could have been handled better…not said things one later regretted.

Who are your role models? Why?

I have learnt various lessons, imbibed many qualities from many of my bosses and superiors. My first boss was fair; he created a meritocracy in the organization. I tried to emulate that. Another boss was a big picture man. He could paint a picture that excited us… make us realize that we were taking tiny steps towards a larger goal.

ARNAB MITRA

'Leaders must follow what they preach': DMITRY SHUKOV,

CEO, MTS INDIA

Dmitry Shukov, CEO of MTS India, does not mind getting his hands dirty, if it helps his team and the company achieve the objective of being a loved and respected telecom operator. Trained at Saint Petersburg Military Telecommunication Academy, Shukov is a keen learner of the market and its dynamics. He jumps into a pool or goes for a jog to relive stress and gets back to drawing board to tackle complex issues of the telecom industry. In an interview Shukov said that he wants to lead by example. Excerpts:

How have you motivated your team to achieve a break-even target in 2014?

The main target for the company is to break even by the fourth quarter of 2013–2014. I have told my team that we will do everything to achieve this target. In fact, the process has already begun. My efforts are focused to help teams bring in efficiency of operation for revenue growth, which also includes cutting down on non-priority operational expenses. It has been my endeavour to make our dealers, retailers and vendors a close-knit family. I constantly meet my teams and not just the leaders to motivate them to achieve the break-even goal.

Spectrum management is a complex issue. What does it take to make every employee appreciate its value?

I believe in a lot of discussion, especially about this issue. As you say here 'brain-storming'. I encourage my team to think out of box when it comes to spectrum management. It has helped in the launch of our state-of-the-art 3G Plus Network. Only innovation will help take us forward our plan to efficiently utilize the fourth carrier (additional spectrum needed by us).

What qualities help you to remain motivated?

It is not easy. Take for example, when the Indian government did not auction 800 MHz, the planning team was disappointed. I told them, let us look at each block, so we first went to the regulator to discuss and understand the issues. Then we went to government to find out why it was done. If you look at the issue from all the stakeholders' position, you will appreciate each aspect and the effort that goes in to understand them. Motivation for me is to understand the point of others and then share my point also.

Do you believe that motivation can be cultivated among others?

Certainly yes, across all the nine circles of our operations, we have recently launched mPower. I strongly believe that ideas for improving MTS India should come from people who are part of the systems and processes—they know the company, the issues and also how to fix them. Within two weeks of the launch of mPower, we already have fifty viable ideas that can potentially make a huge difference in our business performance.

How do you walk the talk?

It is very important for any leader to practice what you preach. My response to an innovation is as quick as I expect my circle chief to respond. In fact, all employees are encouraged to bring about efficiencies in their respective work areas and also be aware on how can they add value to crossfunctionally.

Do you play any sports? What leadership qualities do you like in that sport?

I believe a fit mind resides in a fit body. To keep fit, I love to swim and jog. They are big stress relievers. When you take part in physical activities, it helps to clear your mind and then get back to tackling issues at hand.

Who is the author who inspires you? What book do you like?

I have several favourite authors. One of them is Jack London. His book *Love of Life* and also some of his other stories, published way back in 1907, have been a big source of inspiration. Talking of *Love of Life*, that particular story very well brings out the point that the will to win is the most important thing for any person.

What is the special leadership quality that your employees identify with?

Leadership by example is something I strongly believe in. If a leader expects his team to act in a certain way, then he or she should be at the forefront demonstrating the same traits. This is true not only when it comes to dealing with strategic issues but also the usual operational issues—something as mundane as coming to work on time and being courteous, among other things.

As a leader you have to take tough calls? How do you approach such situations?

Taking tough calls is part of both life and business. I always ask myself—is this necessary for a larger good? If the answer is 'yes' then it brings clarity in making decisions. What is also equally important is that there has to be no compromises when it comes to integrity and ethics.

M RAJENDRAN

'Reinvent yourself and the business every few years': RAHUL JOHRI,

EXECUTIVE VICE-PRESIDENT AND GENERAL MANAGER, SOUTH ASIA, DISCOVERY NETWORKS ASIA-PACIFIC

Executive vice-president and general manager, South Asia, Discovery Networks Asia-Pacific, Rahul Johri joined Discovery in 2001 in the ad sales division. Since then, he has been promoted through the organization. He pioneered the channel's localization drive in India and launched multiple language feeds across different brands. Most recently, he oversaw the successful launch of Discovery Kids in India. He spoke on a range of issues on leadership in an interview. Excerpts:

How do you define a leader?

A leader is the force who creates, drives and reflects the values of the company. A leader is defined by humility in both thoughts and actions.

What are the three most important traits of a leader?

The most critical trait in a leader is that he/she should be able to drive passion in the organization. Next would be the ability to create an environment of trust. Equally important is the resilience and creativity to manage complexities.

As a leader of your group, how do you cultivate leaders?

One of the key approaches I have used to create leaders is empowerment. Once the performance benchmarks are agreed upon, I let the team drive projects with my complete support.

How can a manager become a leader?

Any motivated individual can be nurtured into a leader by demonstrating confidence, consistency and reward.

What is the role of a professional leader in a promoter-driven company?

Around the world, some of the biggest and most successful companies are led by promoters. Today's business intricacies demand that leaders in promoter-driven firms create the finest working atmosphere though a combination of transparency, accountability and admiration.

Since September 2008, the world has fallen into a maelstrom of serial crises. What is the role of a leader in these times?

Leadership needs to evolve in response to political, economic and changing business environment. The economic crisis in 2008 was a big test for business leaders around the world. Ideas that saved the business yesterday are now considered case studies for the future. During a crisis, it is important for the leader to keep the focus on the long-term strategy of the company, while continuing to meet short-term goals. His ability to retain and grow the right talent in the organization becomes even more important during times of crisis.

What has been the biggest leadership challenge you've faced?

The biggest leadership challenge for any CEO is the success with which he/she can retain top talent.

Of late, do you think the role of business leaders has come under the cloud?

Business leaders' performance was always rated on the highest parameters and rightly so. With the emergence of social media, leaders' behaviour and beliefs outside the workplace are as critical.

Leaders have to often carry the cross of other's inefficiencies. What can good leadership do to counterbalance this image?

A leader is responsible for the organization's success and failure in equal measure. Creating transparency across the organization and across levels is the best approach to ascribe accountability.

Your one line leadership mantra?

Embrace change. Reinvent yourself and the business every few years.

Who are the leaders who have inspired you?

I am inspired by Mahatma Gandhi for his belief in 'you must be the change you wish to see in the world.'

Who is a leader in your industry whom you respect?

I drive my inspiration more from ideas than people because I believe that successful ideas have many masters and are often not the creation of an individual, as we often tend to declare. It is more valuable to admire the journey of a brand, product or idea from all counts than restrict to an individual's contribution.

What is the biggest leadership lesson that you have learnt?

I wish I had done everything I did a year in advance. India offers a great opportunity, of course riddled with complications, which Discovery is ideally poised to realize.

What is the best leadership decision you have taken?

My decision to enhance Discovery's channel portfolio in India allowed everyone's role and contribution in the company to grow. The satisfaction of expanding the Indian TV landscape by introducing new genres and redefining existing ones such as Kids and High Definition is unmatched.

GAURAV CHOUDHURY

'A leader must be able to drive change': SAUGATA GUPTA,

CEO, MARICO LTD

From a business based on a single commodity—edible oil—Marico has evolved into a consumer goods company with a solid presence in skincare, health and food segments. Meanwhile, its turnover grew two-and-a-half times in the past five years through diversification and acquisitions in India and abroad. Saugata Gupta, CEO, Marico Ltd, in an interview said that a leader must be proactive and spot things in the environment and drive change in terms of being a thought leader. Excerpts:

How do you define a leader?

A leader has to have the capacity to envision and have an imagination. He has to have the ability to spot and drive change. A leader has to be a game changer; he can't be just a follower and be reactive. He has to be proactive and spot things in the environment and drive change in terms of being a thought leader in the industry. There are short-term and long-term challenges, and therefore, a leader has to have an ability to take calculated risks while being decisive, and I would also say the ability to make sharp choices. A leader needs to be a great communicator.

What are the most important traits of a leader?

What is really important in today's world is impeccable governance and integrity because with all the greed and governance issues, I think a leader has to have very high standards of governance and integrity. He has to be a role model because people look up to him. A leader must manage much more volatility and ambiguity now. He needs to have resilience and ability to constantly change. Lastly, I think a leader has to be humble.

As a leader of your company, how do you cultivate leaders?

We firmly believe that you first need to have the right attitude and values. Skills can always be developed. People coming from premium business schools have a set of skills in any case. But you can't be a completely process-oriented person and say that I'll succeed in marketing. You need to be a very good listener and connect with people. In the first few years, you have to have that hunger for learning new things. We try to give challenging and rotate multiple roles as we develop some of our top talents. The other thing we are trying to do is to bring a change in culture; how to create an environment where failures are okay.

Can leadership be learnt? In other words, how can a manager become a leader?

I think the environment helps quite a bit. Therefore, how you are coached or mentored matters. There are certain core skills or competencies that are important. If you have great coaching and mentoring, you can develop leaders. Having said that there are certain inherent skills, for example, how good you are with people. Emotional intelligence can be developed but not beyond a point. So it is a mix of both.

What is the role of a leader in times of economic crisis?

It is important how I ensure that my long-term goals are not compromised. We need to balance short and long-term pressures. As an FMCG (fast moving consumer goods) company, we have to invest in long-term innovation of products and talent. Suppose there are cost pressures and there are a lot of other costs you can manage but you don't cut innovation and talent.

What has been the biggest leadership challenge you've faced?

If you look at our portfolio 6–7 years ago, it was a branded commodity we were selling. We were not given status of a pure blue-blooded FMCG.

How do you drive the change from branded commodity to value-added products?

Getting into new things and the ability to make aggressive acquisitions were big challenges.

How do you drive change in the organization and how to move up the value chain were big challenges. Do you think the role of business leaders has come under a cloud—globally and domestically—of late?

As long as personal values are strong and you have strong governance, these kind of incidences can be checked. The need is to have strong governance and a risk-management process. That is why people are talking about conscious capitalism as opposed to just making profits.

What is your one line leadership mantra?

If you build capability ahead of growth, the results will come. If I want or take a cricket analogy, I like the 'Rahul Dravid School of Cricket'. It is okay to be boringly consistent and achieve superior results.

MANU P TOMS

'Good leaders identify opportunities early': LEO PURI,

MANAGING DIRECTOR, UTI ASSET MANAGEMENT CO.

Leo Puri, managing director, UTI Asset Management Co., who was previously a director at consultancy McKinsey & Co. and MD with private equity firm Warburg Pincus, took charge as UTI's MD in August last year. Puri said that there is a need to revitalize the organization and feels a good leader will always be able to appreciate and identify opportunities early and mobilize the institution around it. Excerpts from an interview:

How do you define a leader?

I think, leaders are born out of a certain context, there is no one type of leader or leadership style that is necessarily appropriate. A good leader fundamentally responds to the context in which he finds himself.

The context, for example in which we find ourselves, is one where we are in need of renewal and re-energizing. And that calls for requirement to rebuild self-belief, along with laying out a very clear aspiration and creating conviction that is within our grasp. Leadership is also about understanding opportunities and seizing opportunities. People often assume that leadership is about positional power. That is a very low definition of leadership. Leadership is fundamentally about give me an opportunity and let me try and execute it.

What are the key qualities of a leader?

A good leader will always be able to anticipate where opportunities might lie, identify them early enough and mobilize an institution around those. If you can't find opportunities, you really can't exercise leadership. I think it is very hard for me to conceive of what it means to be a leader, when all you are doing is maintaining a status quo. Then you are fundamentally an administrator. So to me, clarity around opportunities, pursuit of opportunities is a hallmark of leadership. Judgements and ability to make good judgements is again the one eternal principle, I think any leader must carry. And he must be willing to be tested on those judgements. I think leaders who adopt authoritarian style of leadership, which refuse to be questioned, are not in my view good leaders.

As a leader, how do you identify and cultivate leaders?

If you are going to develop leaders, you must be able to identify the opportunities and get them to share the aspiration that you have for the institution, so then they help achieve those opportunities. Leadership is also concomitant with the ability to see yourself developing. It can't occur if you are simply stagnant. I clearly believe that you develop leaders not through positional power, but by offering opportunities.

You joined UTI at a time when the company didn't have a proper head for about two years. Being a legacy organization, how difficult is it to change mindset, improve the overall morale and drive the company in such a scenario?

It is not easy, but it is not at all impossible. You have to build on the strengths the institution has. In our case, we do have strengths based on loyalty, love for the institution, good functional skills and capabilities and a sense of pride that goes along with all of that. Yes it is true that compared with some of our competitors, we have lacked the flexibility, the agility, elements of the meritocracy, and therefore on those dimensions, if we are going to become professional meritocracy, we have quite a long way to go. I think you can only solve a problem, by saying, what is it that you start with.

As a managing director, how have you driven through the tough times the financial services industry has faced?

At this point, the role is to revitalize and rebuild. So the focus is on understanding and tapping into our sources of strength. We have spent time to rebuild conviction and self belief, which has to be the foundation of any subsequent change effort. And that has been a priority to remind that we have got the skills and convictions. The challenge continues to be to alter the momentum of the institution, we need to pick up the pace, because if the institution falls into inertia, that is obviously a downward spiral.

What is your one line leadership mantra?

I would say trust, but verify.

NACHIKET KELKAR

'A good leader must be compassionate': SWATI PIRAMAL,

VICE-CHAIRPERSON, PIRAMAL ENTERPRISES

Swati Piramal, the vice-chairperson of Piramal Enterprises, the healthcare to financial services group, says a leader must walk the talk. Even a leader may not know everything, but a good leader must be open to learning, she feels. Piramal spoke on various leadership aspects and said a leader must encourage innovation, which will not only help the company grow but also groom future leaders. Excerpts from an interview:

How do you define a leader?

A leader encourages expertise and innovation. A leader doesn't know everything, but he/she encourages a team process, in which expertise is built. A leader acts on that knowledge. Like you can't say that you know everything but nothing can be done. The leader has to act and do things. And whatever he does, he must have humility. You don't know answers to everything, but anyone who has humility is open to learning more and understanding things. And lastly, a leader must be compassionate.

What are key traits of a leader?

First is integrity, the consistency to walk the talk. Then, its knowledge and the ability to gain knowledge. Thirdly, a good leader has to be humble and caring.

How do you identify and groom future leaders?

The demographic of India makes it so easy. Its stunning to see the talent that we have in our country. The talent is not hard to find, they just need a little grooming, making sure their talk and walk is the same, making sure that what they say, they deliver.

Can leadership be learnt?

Yes. We learn all the time from other great leaders. How did they do things, why did they do things in a certain way? My iconic woman is Drew Faust, head of Harvard University. She is the president of ten schools of Harvard, of which I am on the board. When I see her I feel very inspired, by how one human being can understand the cutting edge of every subject right from environment to climate change to education to science.

As a leader of a company, how would you motivate people to drive innovation?

In our company, we have three values—knowledge, action and care. Under knowledge, we have expertise and innovation. You must have deep knowledge of your subject. The trouble today is that in many areas, people only have superficial knowledge. So we encourage our people to have a lot of training and a lot of deep expertise, in whichever subject, whether its manufacturing, accounts or legal, in whatever they do, they have to be on the top of the game. The other thing is innovation. It's not just product innovation. It could be the way of doing things, the way of thinking about a solution to a problem. We have something called 'manthan', which means churning. Every process gets churned, looking at ways, looking at how to save money.

How difficult has it been as a leader in recent times, since we have gone through a series of financial crises globally?

We did the Abbott deal (sale of healthcare solutions business by Piramal) just before price control was heavily imposed on the Indian pharmaceutical industry. We found ourselves during the time when everyone else was short of money, we had a lot to invest. If you have a war chest you can invest in a very good company. And because the economy is in doldrums, with a strong war chest we could find partners to invest in. Some people take that as opportunity, some take it as a challenge. For us it was a great opportunity to expand and create value for our shareholders.

What is the most challenging decision that you have had to take?

There have been several instances, where I have had to take tough decisions. But one thing I was sure about was our values. If you follow the values, they could never go wrong. Once, three children died after taking Vitamin A, somewhere in Orissa and the Food and Drug Administration stopped my plant, saying children had died taking my vaccine. I told FDA that I had checked my batch, and knew there was nothing wrong with the quality and urged them to go and find the real reason. It turned out that the lady who was feeding the kids had put pesticide in a vitamin A bottle in the kitchen of that primary school and someone mixed up the bottles.

It was eventually found, but sometimes you have to face the angry parents and angry policemen at your doorstep, saying that you have done something wrong. But I was very confident about my people.

What is your one line leadership mantra?

Knowledge, action and care.

NACHIKET KELKAR